LOVE YOURSELF DEEPLY

Self-Love For Women, Recognize Your Self-Worth, Glow With Self-Confidence, Get Your Self-Esteem Back

REBECCA COLLINS

DISCLAIMER

The content contained within this book may not be reproduced, duplicated or transmitted without direct written permission from the author or the publisher.

Under no circumstances will any blame or legal responsibility be held against the publisher, or author, for any damages, reparation, or monetary loss due to the information contained within this book. Either directly or indirectly. You are responsible for your own choices, actions, and results.

<u>**Legal Notice:**</u>

This book is copyright protected. This book is only for personal use. You cannot amend, distribute, sell, use, quote or paraphrase any part, or the content within this book, without the consent of the author or publisher.

<u>**Disclaimer Notice:**</u>

Please note the information contained within this document is for educational and entertainment purposes only. All effort has been executed to present accurate, up to date, and reliable, complete information. No warranties of any kind are declared or implied. Readers acknowledge that the author is not engaging in the rendering of legal, financial, medical or professional advice. The content within this book has been derived from various sources. Please consult a licensed professional before attempting any techniques outlined in this book.

By reading this document, the reader agrees that under no circumstances is the author responsible for any losses, direct or indirect, which are incurred as a result of the use of the information contained within this document, including, but not limited to, — errors, omissions, or inaccuracies.

CONTENTS

INTRODUCTION

Once upon a time, the only way for a woman to find happiness was when a handsome prince came along on a white horse. Saving her from a life of misery, they would then both ride off into the sunset to live happily ever after in a kingdom far, far away. The end.

Unfortunately, that's not quite how it works, as you well know, and times have changed since the days when we were waiting to be rescued, thankfully! Life is far from being a fairy tale and women have now 'almost' reached equality with men in terms of legal, social, and economic status in most parts of the world.

So why do we still feel that we aren't lovable enough, good enough, or worthy enough in our own right?

That's a great question and it needs a very long answer. But this book isn't about the 'whys'.

It's more about the 'hows': how to begin to nurture self-love, boost your self-esteem, grow your confidence and value yourself more. Think of it as a complete makeover from the inside out.

As women, we have all experienced self-doubt, a lack of confidence, and feelings of vulnerability at some point in our lives. Whether it's because of how we look, how much we weigh, what others think of us, or how we are treated, it seems like we are constantly dragging ourselves down in one way or another.

As an entrepreneur who runs workshops to help women get into business, I often hear the same old story: A woman manages to succeed, becomes financially independent, and excels at what she does, possibly even while raising a family. Yet still, she finds herself experiencing bouts of low self-esteem, doubting her abilities, and constantly fretting over her outward appearance.

Most of us are expected to fill many roles from a young age and often, the bar is set at 'perfection'. We should be the perfect daughter, sister, girlfriend, wife, mother, lover, partner, colleague, and friend. Perfection is a lot to achieve when you are only human. No one is capable of that, yet we constantly strive to fit into that mould, and guess what... we are our worst critics!

There is nothing worse than loathing yourself and feeling like you are failing to live up to the standards set by someone else, or by society as a whole. When you dislike yourself, you are always going to feel unfulfilled, no matter what you achieve. This creates so many negative perceptions and stops you from enjoying everything that life has to offer or from reaching your full potential.

It's obvious that being a good mother, achieving professional success, or possessing great beauty doesn't bring inner happiness. They are all admirable qualities for sure, but if you don't love yourself enough, you will never feel that sense of completeness. Self-love is at the heart of this and much more important than your bank balance, your social status, or how attractive you are.

What do I mean when I talk about self-love?

You could be misled into thinking I am suggesting that you become more selfish or indulgent. That couldn't be further from the truth. There are enough of those kinds of people in the world. In effect, self-love is an essential part of human nature and is not only a survival technique but also what we use to grow, mature, and develop. It's as important as breathing and essential for your emotional health. We are all capable of it and not only that: we need to practice it.

I believe that we women have an infinite capacity for love and you see evidence of that every day when you look around you. We are brave when defending our own, valiant when fighting for others, and extremely compassionate and caring. And yet, many of us don't apply that same energy internally.

How often have you gone out of your way to help someone but don't even consider the fact that you may be neglecting yourself? You probably have many role models and wish that you could be like them but how about aspiring to be the best version of you?

In a world obsessed with social media, it's extremely easy to fall into the trap of comparing yourself to other women and I totally get that. Who doesn't wish they were prettier, smarter, richer, or whatever? It's very hard to avoid being pulled into that trap of measuring yourself against others all the time. But when you have achieved the right balance of emotional self-love, those external triggers shouldn't detract from your overall sense of worth.

Here's the thing: It isn't a man's world.

Maybe it used to be, but a lot has changed. This book isn't about how to adopt masculine traits or behavior in order to find happiness. Quite the opposite; it's about embracing who you are as a woman and finding your inner balance based on your terms. It's about setting your own bar. As a woman, you are incredible and capable of doing whatever you set your mind to, so I'm not going to keep using men as a yardstick.

You are a person in your own right and don't need to be defined by others. This is one of the main reasons why you may be suffering from low self-esteem and feelings of not being good enough. If you believe that you have to live up to someone else's expectations, you will never quite make the grade. Other reasons for your low self-esteem and lack of self-love may have a lot to do with your past, any negative or traumatic experiences, an unhappy childhood, or a toxic relationship that stops you from being happy with yourself.

It's possible that you feel inadequate as a mother, incompetent as a boss, useless as a partner, or worthless as a person. That is not a happy place to be and unless you do something about it, there could be long-term effects on your physical health and mental well-being. It all begins in that place deep within you which I call your *mind mirror*.

Your *mind mirror* reflects whatever you tell it to. Feeling inferior? Unloved? Inadequate? Unworthy? Any thoughts that you use to describe yourself are reflected in that mirror, causing you to believe that what you see is a true impression of yourself. This distorted image you have created has become your reality, making it difficult for you to find a sense of inner contentment. It's time to smash that mirror and learn how to create a true image of yourself, one in which your values, qualities, and abilities shine through.

Whatever the reasons for your inability to fully love yourself (and some of them may seem very complex), in this book you will learn how to overcome them.

You will nurture a greater appreciation for who you are.

You will read about practical strategies to help you overcome your negative self-perceptions.

You will discover ways to boost your self-esteem.

You will unlock the secrets to genuine happiness.

As you go through each chapter, you will begin to recognize what true inner beauty is and understand how to nurture that. You will find practical tips on how to develop a positive inner voice and silence that inner critic. There are strategies for letting go of self-sabotaging thoughts and shame associated with your physical appearance. You will gain insights into why making yourself a priority is so empowering and how to cope with toxic relationships. Each chapter comes with its own set of daily affirmations that you can incorporate into your mindset and there is even a journal at the end of the book for you to jot down your thoughts, feelings, and goals.

Practicing self-love means understanding and accepting your flaws, being aware of the good within you, and recognizing your authentic self. Share as much love as you want with the world, but you have to begin with your own needs first. That's exactly what this book will help you to accomplish and through it, you will learn that beauty isn't really skin deep. It is an immense source of joy that is waiting to be unleashed within you and all you need to do is open up to that possibility.

No matter at which stage you are in your life, it's never too late to reframe that mirror and see a different person but it has to begin with getting rid of old habits, misconceptions, self-sabotaging thoughts and negative attitudes.

Begin today and as you turn each page of this book, you will discover a woman who is worthy of love, respect, admiration, and compassion.

Yes, that woman is you!

<u>**Free for you.**</u>

10 Weekly Issues of Rebecca's life-changing news-letter "Reclaim Your Power" Rebecca covers Self Love, Self Esteem, Making Friends, Getting Your Life Back & Living A Life of Freedom.

https://rebecca.subscribemenow.com/

HOW DO I LOVE MYSELF AS A WOMAN?

"A girl should be two things: who and what she wants."
– Coco Chanel

Self-love starts with the recognition and appreciation of our inner worth and value.

When I was ten years old, my mother commented that I was so plain I could transform myself into whatever I wanted when older. I think she meant it as some kind of compliment as she went on to say, "Your hair is such a drab color that you can go blonde, be a redhead, do highlights... anything at all." Despite her 'flattery', I took her remarks very badly. Even at that age, I had this feeling I wasn't good enough the way I was and had to be something else. Well, 'had to' is a strong term, but hey, if your own mother thinks you need a makeover, who are you to argue?

Growing up in a family with four brothers didn't help. Actually, the last thing on my mind was what my hair looked like. I was more interested in being as tough as them, not crying when thumped, and able to climb trees just as high as they did in some bizarre act of macho bravado. I honestly believed that I was as good as them, even faster than one or two of them, and a lot smarter. What I didn't understand was why, as a girl, *I needed to be prettier and should focus more on what I looked like, not on what I could do.* It didn't seem to matter that I was top of my class in school, a 100-meters track champion, and a good kid. I had to be prettier.

I am sure that your life experience is completely different from mine, but you will get my point. Growing up, it struck me that girls and women are usually judged not on their abilities but on how they look, first and foremost. Today, living in a liberated society where gender equality and freedom of expression are actively encouraged and promoted, I got to wondering why it is then that all of the studies show women continue to experience more self-doubt than men.

Why can't we just love ourselves for what we are?

Perhaps it goes back to the "You can even be a blonde..." dialogue, which is a narrative buried deep somewhere in our feminine psyches. Your experience may be one of "you should be thinner," or "you should be sexier." Whatever it is, there is something about being a woman that includes the maxim that we aren't good enough. Good enough for who?

You could say that it all began back in the days when patriarchy first established itself. I don't want to bore you with ancient history or go on a feminist rant. But interestingly enough, there was a time way before civilization as we know it developed when women did have equal standing with men, and society wasn't divided into roles based on 'he' and 'she'. I think the move away from that lies at the crux of everything we have been experiencing ever since as women — trying to feel self-validated on our own terms and being capable of loving ourselves, flaws and all.

Around 10000 BCE in the Andes, a very primitive hunter-gatherer society was organized around who does what best and not what gender you were. Despite the myth of the big, hairy, male hunter bringing home dinner to the starving, helpless family, it has been discovered that women were also fine hunters. Whether they were faster, more agile, or perhaps better shots, it matters not. They were just as capable and useful as men and I doubt that they had any issues with self-doubt. I would imagine that if you were appreciated for your survival skills and contribution to the community, you wouldn't have any issues with low self-esteem (just saying...).

Three thousand years later, when the first semi-agrarian communities were beginning to develop in the plains of Anatolia, once again we discover that society was pretty gender-neutral. That is, everyone pitched in and did what they were good at for the benefit of the tribe or clan. We find a lot of evidence of that in the ancient city of Çatalhöyük (pronounced 'chah-tahl-hu-yook') in modern-day southern Turkey. After that, well, things got a bit one-sided when the powers that be began to restrict women to domestic duties, and their identity was linked to being a wife and mother.

You may be wondering what all of this has to do with self-love. Surely, we have come a long way since the days when women were seen merely as sexual objects and classed as property or had no say over their sexual reproduction. Em... those points actually sound very current if you think about it. But yes, you are right, we have come a long way and certainly feel more empowered today.

Here's the thing: it takes a very, very long time to undo how history has taught us to be. You may know who you are, but your experience today carries with it centuries of inherited preconceptions, enforced behavior patterns, and emotional parameters. Men are not to blame for how we feel about ourselves and we are all responsible for creating a society based on mutual respect and equality. When you put things into perspective, it appears that we are still trying to catch up psychologically with our legal, economic, and political emancipation. So if you struggle with self-love, it's really not surprising.

Now, if we look at why so many women today have issues like low self-esteem, a lack of confidence, and little self-compassion, it is probably because many of us still feel that we should be something else. As I mentioned above, there are many reasons for this but none that we can't deal with. Whether it is the way you were brought up, peer pressure, the culture you were born into, or your life experiences, overcoming stereotypical thought patterns and behavior can be tough.

Let me stop right there and tell you something: you don't have to be anything else other than who you are. You don't need to be a man, a superwoman, the perfect wife, girlfriend, mother, or the Virgin Mary herself. If you look in the Cambridge dictionary for a definition of the word 'woman', it is simply this: *'an adult female human being'*. That's all you have to be.

My rally call to you is to embrace your womanhood, and it all begins with self-love.

Many millennials are facing a number of challenges today: striving to be the best they can be while struggling with those age-old feelings of inadequacy and self-loathing. This is obvious when we look at the damaging effects of social media and the fact that the majority of young women's role models are not bringing anything substantial to the table. Quite the opposite: the fake, superficial, overly-edited lifestyles we are being sold only add to a feeling of inferiority and insecurity. If you belong to the older generation of women who lived through the feminist movement of the 60s and 70s, you may be asking why we still need to set a date aside each year to celebrate *International Women's Day*. Surely, if feminism had been successful, we wouldn't need a dedicated 'let's remember how special we are' day. The *#Me Too* movement has also highlighted a lot of ingrained behaviors held by those in powerful or influential positions, and just when we thought it was safe to show our feminine side, we are accused of provoking sexual violence. Clearly, we still have a long way to go.

A recent study by The Body Shop called *The Body Shop Self-Love Index* identified a global self-love crisis amongst women, with 60% of those involved in the survey wishing they had more respect for themselves. Over 22,000 people of different ages, gender, and living standards in 21 different countries took part and were asked about their levels of self-worth, wellbeing, and happiness. Some of the factors that seemed to affect the self-love rankings were the frequent use of social media, being single, anxiety and depression, belonging to a minority group, being under 35, financial status, and world events (e.g. politics, the economy).

If the study is anything to go by, it gives us a pretty good idea of how badly women feel about themselves. Funnily enough, similar studies carried out on men reveal that they too have issues with self-esteem and the difference in percentages is fractional, which tells us that we aren't the only ones to experience self-doubt or feelings of worthlessness. Bearing that in mind, I don't want to characterize women as weak or conflicted by their very nature, but more that they internalize external events in a completely different way to men. This is good to know because it means that we are capable of rewiring our responses and unlearning negative thinking to create a much healthier mindset.

To do so, we need to examine how we feel about ourselves and then apply strategies to elevate our levels of self-love. I want you to start by taking a look at the statements below and noting how much you agree or disagree with each one on a scale of 1 to 5. Just respond without thinking too much about it and afterward, you can get a better idea of which areas you need to focus on.

Rank your response based on the following scale:

1 = Disagree completely

2 = Disagree a little

3 = Agree somewhat

4 = Mostly agree

5 = Agree completely

Are you ready? OK, here goes:

1. I hate myself
2. I am dissatisfied with who I am
3. I want to be perfect
4. I hate my body
5. I feel worthless
6. I am overly sensitive
7. I feel anxious
8. I feel angry
9. I feel insecure
10. I want to please people
11. I make a lot of mistakes

How well did you do?

Even if you disagree with most of the above statements, I am sure that you lingered a little longer on at least one of them. I am even going to take an educated guess and say that you probably strongly agree with two or three of them. That is perfectly understandable because when there is an absence of self-love, you tell yourself you are lacking in some way. It's a dialogue that you are reinforcing every time you say things like, "I'm too sensitive," or "I wish I was thinner."

- When you hate yourself or feel frustrated with who you are, you will find it very hard to forgive yourself for even the smallest hiccups or mistakes. This compounds your belief that you are unlovable — you don't even love yourself, so how could anyone else love you? That's an extremely self-destructive pattern of thought, isn't it?
- When you feel that you need to be perfect all the time, it can eat away at your self-esteem because you are setting yourself totally unrealistic goals. Failure is part of life and if your end goal is perfection, you'll find failure very difficult to handle.
- Hating your body is also extremely detrimental to your sense of overall well-being and if you are always comparing your butt size to others, you will never, ever be happy in your own skin.
- If you believe that you have nothing useful to contribute and don't see yourself as having any value, you deny yourself the opportunity to show your abilities and talents. And don't forget: when you tell yourself that you are worthless, this is exactly what you are projecting to others around you.
- Buying into the idea that you are overly sensitive is also stunting you because you are less likely to stand your ground and be proactive in life. There is nothing wrong with being sensitive, as long as it isn't used as an excuse for being apathetic and easily manipulated.
- Wanting to please people is a very altruistic pursuit, but often done for the wrong reasons and at great

cost. It may make you feel validated and appreciated but you shouldn't need external approval to feel good about yourself. Being able to establish limits and saying 'no' more often is a sign of self-respect, not selfishness.

If you identify with any of the above points, you may find it extremely difficult to practice self-love because you have such a low estimation of yourself. I wonder how easy it is for you to make the following statements instead and begin to believe in them:

I have a high regard for my own well-being and happiness.

I see to my own needs and don't sacrifice my well-being to please others.

I don't settle for less than I deserve.

On being beautiful

Women are intrinsically beautiful. They have the power to create life and give boundless love. From a purely aesthetic point of view, they may be deemed beautiful or not, depending on the cultural norms of the day. One minute, Kate Moss is the paradigm of perfection and before you know it, large derrières are back as a symbol of femininity. These are all subjective notions that are reflected in a specific cultural era and we only have to look at how women have been portrayed throughout the history of art to understand that perceptions of beauty change over time.

Everyone has their own unique beauty, and the idea that you have to have a certain skin tone, nose shape, or body type is absolutely ridiculous when you think about it. Mainstream media may wish to tell you otherwise, but why buy into the hype? All that does is cause you unnecessary pain and anguish as you strive to be someone you are not. Embracing your outward appearance is an essential step towards self-love, which means being able to look in the mirror without judging yourself. Instead of staring at your reflection and making a mental wish list of all the things you want to change, try telling yourself how beautiful you are.

"Self-affirming habits are your greatest weapon because the more you tell yourself how wonderful you are, the more you will begin to believe it."

More than just a pretty face

Beauty isn't defined only by how you look. What's more, the longer you linger on the physical aspects, the less attention you will pay to the internal qualities you possess. It's such a pity to spend all of your time worrying about whether or not you meet the current 'beauty' standards and prevent the amazing potential within you from shining through. Beauty can be an action, a thought, a gesture, a passion, a talent, a viewpoint, and once you realize that, you will begin to nurture a much healthier level of self-esteem.

Ask anyone for their definition of beauty, and you will get a range of answers, from the way someone smiles to how they treat others. There is a whole spectrum of 'being beautiful' and it doesn't start and stop with your face or body. Even though you want to look your best, start to explore aspects of your inner beauty and forget about your waistline for a while. We will take a more detailed look at body issues (I am sure you have some) later on in Chapter 4.

Trending now

We are living in an era where inclusivity is becoming the norm. The world is a much smaller place now, thanks to technology and the internet, and everyone is invited to do their thing, express their sexuality, and be 'diverse'. Fashion is a free-for-all where anything goes and you can be however and whoever you want to be, with cosmetic surgery also offering a helping hand. That's all great! But in the buzz surrounding our image, we are ignoring other aspects of beauty that are much more qualitative and meaningful.

You could feel quite satisfied with your appearance, and still be lacking in confidence and that's because we are still judging a book by its cover to a large extent. I'm all for dressing how you like and expressing your personality with your tattoos, weird hair-do, or piercings, but at the end of the day, it is still an outward display and has nothing to do with inner self-worth.

I want you to think about some characteristics that you admire in other women. They could be well-known personalities, friends, or family members. Use some of the words below to describe what makes them beautiful in your eyes:

Kind

Generous

Funny

Compassionate

Caring

Intelligent

Brave

Resourceful

Talented

Creative

You can add to this list...

Now that you have described another woman using some of the above words, which ones would you use to describe yourself? Are you funny, creative, kind? These are all aspects of your inner beauty. You don't have to be a beacon of virtue, have 50,000 followers on Instagram, or be a power-wielding corporate boss. You just have to be you. Instead of trying to fit in with trends or being influenced by people that you don't even know and will probably never meet, seek out positive female role models in your close circle.

When you look at a photograph of your mother, sister, or best friend, what do you see? Do you immediately start to judge their appearance or connect emotionally with the wonderful person that you know? I often look at a photo of my mother taken just before she died at the age of 86. All I can see is a beautiful, kind, intelligent woman who gave me so much love. That's the person I want to see when I look in the mirror and I know that it is within me to do so, just as it is within you. When you can really see that inner beauty, you will have discovered a precious treasure that no one can take away from you because it is intrinsic to you alone.

"You have the potential to love yourself and when you do that, it will inspire others to do the same."

Here are some simple yet effective ways in which you can achieve that:

- **Be passionate**

Women who love themselves exude contentment. They understand what makes them happy and follow their passions. This may sound like a cliché, but if you have a sense of purpose and pursue that to the fullest, you will stop worrying so much about whether your mascara has smudged or not. By all means, take care of your appearance, but don't make it your number one priority. There is more to life than that. When you are involved in doing what you love, everything else fades into insignificance and your brain begins to release 'feel-good' hormones so, the more often you follow your passions, the better.

- **Be compassionate**

If you can't do a Jane Goodall and spend thirty years in the jungle protecting apes, you can still be compassionate every day in small ways. Start off by learning self-compassion first and stop beating yourself up for things that you did or didn't do in the past. Empowerment comes when you learn from mistakes and move forward, not from holding yourself back with regret and self-criticism. Not only will this help you to be stronger, but it will help you to understand others easier and show them the same understanding and empathy.

- **Smarten up**

Intelligence is a very appealing trait that has nothing to do with how many degrees or certificates you have on your wall. It is a skill that enables you to achieve specific results and as you are an intelligent being, you have the capacity to be just as good as the next person. If you feel worthless or not taken seriously enough, it is a great idea to learn some new skills. Not only will this boost your confidence, but it will also help you to achieve more in life. It could be that you decide to take an online course about reiki or start weekly tennis lessons. Whatever it is, it is a positive step to help you to practice greater self-love and begin believing in your abilities.

- **Have fun**

Life is supposed to be enjoyable, so stop taking yourself too seriously. Laughter is a great remedy for anxiety and depression and I want you to find reasons to laugh each day, even if it is at yourself. Loosen up and release yourself from self-criticism and judgment and embrace the lighter side of things instead. Do something that you enjoy more often, such as eating out or going for long walks, and set five minutes aside each day to indulge in a pleasant experience. Whether it's eating your favorite ice cream or putting your feet up, give yourself the chance to experience pleasure because that will leave you feeling restored and pampered.

- **Grow old gracefully**

You can't fight time, so please stop trying. No matter how tempted you are to resent your looks or physical abilities as age begins to make its presence felt, see your life as a celebration instead. Each phase of our lives has its own beauty, challenges, and rewards and there are many women all over the world enjoying life right up to a very grand age. As Sophia Loren once said when asked how she felt about her wrinkles, "They are my lifelines. Why would I want to get rid of them?" Self-love equals self-care and as long as you keep fit and follow a healthy lifestyle, there's no reason why you should feel less than happy at any age.

- **Mind the gap**

You probably spend a large part of your day on auto-pilot: working, raising a family, doing chores, and collapsing into bed at night. We have become accustomed to being constantly busy and spend very little time focusing on our inner selves. If you can take ten minutes each morning or night to sit silently and focus on that moment, it is the equivalent of recharging your smartphone. Why? Because by being mindful, you allow yourself to just 'be'. Without the need to be somewhere else or occupied with other things, you create space for 'you'. In this space, which I call 'the gap', you can reconnect with all of the thoughts and feelings that you push aside as you go through your day. When you do so, you will begin to tap into a deeper personal understanding of who you are.

"To love yourself as a woman requires nothing more than an acceptance of who you are and a desire to enjoy life."

Self-acceptance is the key to liberating yourself from any outside force that may be causing you to feel worthless, undesirable, and unlovable. We are all born with the inherent desire to live life to the fullest — that's our purpose as a species.

Within this brightly colored kaleidoscope of living, there is so much for you to look forward to and nothing stopping you but your own mindset. In the next chapter, we are going to take a look at how your self-esteem can be improved through the power of self-talk. At the moment, that chatter going on inside your head is probably your worst enemy, so we are going to learn how to turn it into your best friend instead.

At the end of each chapter, I am going to give you a unique affirmation that you can use every day. Affirmations are a great way to begin the process of embracing self-love because they act as a positive reinforcement when you may be feeling particularly low or unable to see the light at the end of the tunnel.

Here, it's all about intention: meaning what you say and believing it. As you repeat the affirmation to yourself, say it wholeheartedly and feel the power that it instills you with. You can repeat it 5 times each morning when you wake up or last thing at night in the mirror before going to sleep. Write it down and stick

it on your fridge or pc monitor. However you say it, say it with love!

Affirmation:

I love the person that I am and the person I am becoming.

🏵 2 🏵
SELF-ESTEEM AND
SELF-TALK

"You've been criticizing yourself for years and it hasn't worked. Try
approving of yourself and see what happens."
– Louise Hay

Self-esteem grows when you learn to stop listening to the negative inner voice that prevents you from believing in yourself.

I talk to myself a lot. The conversation is usually a dialogue between the *me* that I love and the *me* that wants to bring me down. Over the years, I've learned to pay much less attention to the latter because it's usually fake news.

When I make a mistake, instead of letting that negative voice tell me what a failure I am, I listen to the more positive voice so that I can put things into a better perspective. If I feel doubt creeping in, rather than spiraling into the 'I'm useless' monologue, I remind myself of my strengths. When I feel low, I avoid licking my emotional wounds and recall some of the things I have achieved in my life. This kind of self-talk helps me to boost my confidence and the belief in my abilities, filling me with a healthy level of self-esteem. It's something I have learned to apply no matter what the circumstances and you could say that my inner voice is my best friend.

We all engage in self-dialogue, although many of us are stuck in a pattern of having a negative conversation with someone who thinks the worst of us. This negative inner voice is an expert at pointing out weaknesses, faults, and imperfections, and it does it all the time. As women, we are masters of this habit and are the first ones to criticize ourselves or be judgmental. We do it so well that we don't need to hear it from anyone else. Here's a good example: someone pays you a compliment today by saying how nice you look in your new dress. What do you do? Rather than saying, "Thank you," and leaving it at that, you are more likely to reply with something like, "Thanks, but do you think it's too tight?" or, "thanks, but I feel so fat in it." The inability to accept a compliment gracefully isn't your way of seeking flattery. It's you telling yourself that you don't deserve the compliment and you would rather settle for a negative remark.

Most of our interactions are based on how we feel about ourselves and if you ooze self-confidence, you will take praise or positive feedback in your stride. But if you lack that sense of worth, you will be constantly telling yourself that you are too fat, too short, too old, too young, or *too anything* and no amount of well-intentioned words are going to make you believe otherwise. Your inner critic rules and when it tells you that you are *too anything*, you believe it.

Where is all of this negative self-talk coming from and how can you overcome it? Those are the nitty-gritty questions that I want to talk about in this chapter because what you tell yourself is directly linked to your sense of self-esteem. If self-esteem is the ability to feel good about ourselves, then negative self-talk is a toxic arrow that aims to sabotage that feeling. It wants to burst your bubble and manages to do that pretty well most of the time.

There are many, many reasons why you may lack self-esteem, some of which can be traced back to the way you were brought up. You may have had very demanding parents who were never satisfied with your behavior or academic performance, leaving you feeling inadequate. You could have had neglectful teachers who didn't encourage you or help you to develop self-confidence. Maybe you suffered a traumatic experience or were a victim of abuse, leaving you feeling powerless and unable to control your life. Even if you grew up in a very nurturing family, your self-esteem could have taken a knock after a particular event much later on in life, such as failing some important exams or losing your job. It's possible that you were involved in a romantic relationship that left you feeling rejected or used after it ended.

Like I say, there are an infinite number of variables that could have contributed to the way you feel about yourself today. It will be useful if you take some time to think about anything that you feel has shaped your level of self-esteem and confidence as you were growing up. You probably already have a good idea, but if not, work through it gently and if anything comes up that you are unable to deal with right now, that's also fine. This process may take some time but it is essential if you want to eventually get rid of any baggage from your past that is weighing down your present and future.

Most experts agree that about half of our personality comes from our gene pool and life experiences help to shape the other half. This means that at least 50% of who you are is flexible and can be affected by how you handle life. Basically, you begin with a label of yourself such as 'I'm the weak one in the family' and then you work at fitting your experiences into that mold. This is because your brain works best when it can organize everything into clearly defined boxes so the more you tell yourself you are weak, the more you will seek to reinforce that fact. Of course, it works both ways. If you were constantly hailed as 'the bright kid', then your brain will try to justify that label too whenever it can.

I am sure that you can recall very clearly a negative comment made about you ten years ago yet have great difficulty bringing to mind something positive that you heard in a similar scenario.

No doubt, when your first boyfriend told you that you are fat, that comment was etched into your memory, while you can't remember being told by your second boyfriend that he loves how curvy you are. This has got to do with a thing called **negative bias** and if we were more aware of it, we could make our lives a whole lot easier. When you find yourself fixating on an ill-spoken remark by a friend or keep going over and over your mistakes in your head, it's because negative events impact our brains more than positive ones do. The fancy term for this is positive-negative asymmetry, which basically means that we tend to dwell more on the bad than the good. This explains why it is so difficult for many people to overcome past traumas or forget unpleasant experiences.

It's a human trait, so you don't have to feel bad about it, but it's refreshing to know that we can work on overturning it and focus more on positive experiences rather than negative ones. It all begins when we pay too much attention to these negative soundbites, instead of putting them into a realistic and healthy context.

You know that negative bias is controlling your life when you can relate to the following examples:

- You were supposed to pick up your partner's dry cleaning on the way home but forgot. You feel terrible and remind yourself how unreliable you are and wonder what he/she sees in you.

- You have a row with your best friend and afterward, go over all her flaws, rather than focusing on her positive qualities and remembering how much she means to you.
- You receive your annual job appraisal and, although it's great overall, there are one or two remarks about areas that you need to work on. You fixate on those remarks and go home feeling upset and deflated.
- Your personal trainer tells you that you need to work more on your abs. You take this as meaning you are imperfect, flabby, and never going to get that fabulous beach body, no matter how hard you try.

Do any of those responses sound familiar? It's not surprising if they do, because we are wired that way. Ever since the days when we had to be on a constant state of alert in a world full of threats, we have become used to paying attention to warning signs to ensure survival. It's just the brain's way of making sure we are kept safe and even though we don't need to have that heightened sense of awareness anymore, old habits die hard. The problem is that focusing on the negatives can seriously affect your mental state, well-being, relationships, and decision-making abilities.

We are not going to get rid of that negative bias, but what we can do is shut down that inner voice when it starts to go into overdrive.

The truth is that you are what you think you are and if you see yourself through a negative lens, that is exactly the person you will become. On the other hand, by adopting a positive self-dialogue, you can begin to develop a better self-image, build healthier connections and enjoy life more. It isn't about creating an unrealistic, fantastical image of yourself. It's about self-acceptance, self-esteem, and self-love, and you can begin by using the following strategies:

Shift the narrative

This takes some practice and it's not easy, because you will be so used to listening to that hostile chatter in your head every time you do or say something. Whenever an event occurs, you will automatically start going through what happened and wishing you had said this or done that. As soon as you realize that you are going down that rabbit hole, just stop. You can't change the past — it's gone — so focus instead on how you would handle the same situation in the future. Here's an example of what I mean:

I had invited a few friends around for a Mexican night and wanted to show off my culinary skills. Unfortunately, I added way too much chili powder to the con carne, making it impossible for anyone to eat it. Of course, they all laughed about it in a good-hearted way and said it was no big deal. This could have gone one of two ways: either I immediately tell myself that I am careless, inconsiderate and an extremely bad cook or I laugh about it and make a mental note to ease up on the chili powder next time. If I went down the first road of chastising myself, this would reinforce my existing beliefs that I am careless and make me think twice about organizing such an event again. I will end up telling myself I am incapable and this will have lasting effects on how successful I will be when faced with a future challenge.

A bit over the top? I agree, but that is how our negative thinking works. It joins all the dots together and ultimately controls what you do or don't do in life, affecting your sense of self-worth and your relationships. Bearing that in mind, I prefer to laugh it off and maybe make Italian next time!

Tell a positive story

The way that you describe your life and who you are says a lot about how you shape that perception of yourself. When something 'bad' happens to you, your inner voice may begin telling you that it's all your fault, or that you brought it on yourself. Don't listen to that; most things in life are out of our control and it's the way we react to them that matters, not who is to blame. People who look on the bright side have a much healthier way of dealing with misfortune or mishaps and will learn from any mistakes. They focus on getting back on track and don't sit dwelling on what went wrong but concentrate on making things right. Give your story a happy ending too instead of it being all doom and gloom, because that is exactly how you will feel.

Stop thinking and start doing

Whenever we are physically inactive, our brain starts to take over. It finds all of this empty space to fill so, being a brain, wants to make itself useful. If you find yourself chewing over the past or worrying about the future, then you need to do something in the present. Rather than creating opportunities for negative thoughts to pop up, do something active and be fully engaged in that. It could be anything, from going for a walk to a trip to the local mall. Do whatever it takes to disengage from negative dialogue and you will see the benefits immediately. Physical activity of any kind gets your brain focusing on other functions, leaving you to relax and have some peace from the constant inner critic inside you.

Cherish the present moment

You may be tired of all the hype about mindfulness, but there is a reason why it is so effective. Remember what I said about negative memories staying with us longer than positive ones? What you need to do is reset that balance so that your brain gets used to more positive experiences, which will eventually outweigh the negatives. You can't change what went on in the past but you can certainly take control of your present, and that is a great opportunity to grab those positive vibes. As you begin to stock up your long-term memory with pleasurable memories, the bad things will eventually lose their position in the pecking order. We know that if you take a moment to enjoy something in the now and replay it several times in your mind, it will become embedded in your long-term memory and that's a wonderful resource for moments when your self-esteem is low.

There is an area in your brain that's dedicated to negative thinking called the anterior cingulate cortex and it's very judgemental. It's the part responsible for your emotional reactions and has been built in this way to respond effectively to the needs of others. Some research suggests that, as a woman, this area of your brain is slightly larger than that of a man's, meaning that you come equipped with an extra superpower by design; enhanced emotional sensitivity. This could be a blessing or a curse, depending on your viewpoint. In general, the differences between a man's and a woman's brains are microscopically minute so I don't want to insist that gender and biology make a massive difference here. Suffice to say that if we women tend to react more emotionally than men, this could be a biological characteristic and it could also be linked to several other factors such as how we are brought up, our character, and, of course, social conditioning.

What I can say for certain is that when your inner critic is constantly calling you stupid, unattractive, deeply flawed, and unlovable, that causes a great deal of anxiety and seriously affects your stress levels. If that negative voice is always pointing out perceived flaws and faults, dismissing your achievements, and filling your head with self-hate, it's no wonder that you feel stressed out, emotionally down, or even depressed.

All of the negative feelings that you have ever had about yourself are perpetuated by the myth your thoughts have created surrounding your capabilities and potential.

You are not to blame for that, and criticism is not my intention. What you can do is begin to love yourself and introduce self-dialogue that is compassionate, encouraging, kind, and caring. Think of how you talk to your loved ones — that's the way you should be talking to yourself. Do you chastise them for their mistakes, make discouraging remarks, keep dredging up their past failures and wilfully cause them to feel guilt, shame, or anger? I am sure your answer is a resounding 'NO' so why are you doing that to yourself? Think about it.

Challenge your inner critic

One of the best ways to begin talking to yourself with self-love is to challenge your inner critic. You can do this by giving it a name, or referring to it as a third person. When you stop referring to it as 'I', you disassociate yourself from whatever it says and it begins to lose its power.

Call it whatever you like, but position it so that it's not you talking - it's a third person. Here's an example: instead of saying, "I always choose the wrong guy" (a common self-complaint), reframe that into, "Inner critic says that I always choose the wrong guy." This statement then becomes an opinion — not your opinion, but that of someone else, and gives you leverage to reflect on it and either agree or disagree. You don't have to believe it.

Another example may be when your thoughts tell you, "I'll never be successful in my career, I'll never pass that exam, I'll never find a boyfriend," or whatever.... Don't let those thoughts become written in stone — your inner critic isn't in control of your life, you are. Simply let those thoughts pass by with a response like, "Oh, there goes my inner critic again sounding off." If you can learn to let it have its say without paying too much attention to it, it will soon realize that it doesn't have that much influence over you.

Come in with a strong counter strike whenever you hear those kinds of discouraging remarks with words like. "Hey, I can do this, I am capable, I am worthy." If you want to give your inner critic a name, feel free. Mine is called *Mosquito*; she flits around my head, annoyingly so, and I wave her away whenever she starts to really bother me. I've got to admit, I don't see as much of her as I used to, but when I do feel her buzzing in my ear, I am more than ready to deal with her negative small-talk.

On occasions when I fear that I have made a bad decision or feel guilty about how I treated someone, *Mosquito* pops up, always ready to have her say. I immediately think about my words and actions and if I come to the conclusion that I have indeed made some kind of error or truly caused distress to someone, I find a way to fix it rather than internalizing it. I don't want to be a bad, sad person because it isn't good for me. I don't think you want to put yourself in that position either, and now there is no need to.

Truth versus fiction

I know that you have grown up believing that you are *like this* or *like that* because someone has told you so, and you believed them. It's time to learn how to separate truth from fiction because when you live according to how other people see you, you are not being truthful to yourself.

Words are just words, whether they are coming from an external source or from within. Other people's opinions of you are just that - opinions, and you don't need to accept them as gospel. When words are internal, they represent our beliefs but they aren't facts. You only have to think of someone with an eating disorder who sees an obese person when they look in the mirror, even though their body is dangerously underweight. This kind of distorted belief mechanism is extremely harmful and can cause you to suffer from a lot of mental, emotional, and physical anguish.

By defusing unhelpful thoughts that try to convince you something is true, you will be able to have more clarity about who you really are. There is a big difference between thinking '*I am stupid*' and thinking '*My inner critic says I'm stupid*'. The first one is almost like a reflex or bad habit, and the second one is a result of you distancing yourself from the superficial layers that have been piling up for so long. Take it from me — you are not stupid, so stop believing that you are.

Friend or foe?

Your inner voice is not always working against you. It is the part of your brain that alerts you to danger and tells you that something is not quite right in your environment. The problem comes when you don't have a yardstick by which to measure when it is protecting you and when it's the inner critic kicking in to cause unnecessary suffering. One easy way to tackle this is to stop every time it happens and ask yourself: Is this a person I would like to hang out with or is it someone who is making my life a misery? The inner critic is the latter one and is not someone you would wish to spend much time with. Why would you want to stick with anybody who abuses you, taunts you, and demeans you? I am sure that you wouldn't call that person your friend. A true friend will be honest but kind, compassionate despite your failings, and supportive when you are down.

Change the conversation

There is another very simple trick to deal with your negative self-talk when it arises and that is by changing what is said. You will find some examples below and I can tell you that this is an extremely effective way to win that argument with yourself. Not only will you feel good afterward, but you are helping your brain to make new neural pathways that allow you to embrace self-love.

Example 1

Your negative self-talk: *"I'm such an idiot! I scratched the car when I was parking and now it's ruined."*

Your positive self-talk: *'I shouldn't have tried to park in such a tight spot. I'll avoid doing the same thing in the future and be extra careful next time.'*

Example 2

Your negative self-talk: *"I can't get my head around this new project. I'll never be able to understand it."*

Your positive self-talk: *'This is something new that I need time to digest. I'm sure I will get the hang of it if I go through it again."*

Example 3

Your negative self-talk: *"I don't want to go to the party. I won't know anyone there and will probably end up standing in a corner all night."*

Your positive self-talk: *'It's always nerve-racking meeting new people, but I'm a good conversationalist and I'm sure I'll find someone interesting to talk to.'*

As you can see, it doesn't take much to turn that inner conversation around to something more positive. Even if you only half-heartedly believe what you are saying at first, keep repeating it until it becomes your new reality.

Practice self-compassion

Self-compassion doesn't mean feeling sorry for yourself and saying *poor me*. It is about being caring and loving, just as you would treat your nearest and dearest. Imagine what you would say to a good friend who is struggling with low self-esteem and consider how you would talk to them. Would you be mean and harsh, or understanding and encouraging? This is the way you should talk to yourself, with genuine care and kindness. By forgiving yourself for your blunders and inadequacies, you will nurture a more loving appreciation for all of your qualities and accomplishments.

We women are very good at giving and caring for others but often, we forget about caring for ourselves. This can easily escalate into putting ourselves last or seeing ourselves as less than worthy. If you feel like that, talk to your best friend — the positive person inside you who is just waiting to give you all of the strength and support you need.

Self-esteem is a seed that is embedded deep within you. You only need to water it and make sure it gets plenty of sunshine to grow and flourish.

The steps that you need to take to go from negative self-talk to a place of positive reinforcement are easy to apply, once you set your mind to it. In the next chapter, I want to talk about the self-sabotaging tactics that you may unwittingly use on the way to get there. I'm not going to allow you to set yourself up for failure, so don't even think about it. Take a deep breath in, breathe out and keep going with a brave heart and a mind made up to succeed. You are doing great!

Affirmation:

I choose to use thoughts and feelings that empower me.

❦ 3 ❦
LETTING GO OF SELF-JUDGMENT

"Self-criticism, like self-administered brain surgery, is perhaps not a good idea. Can the 'self' see the 'self' with any objectivity? — Joyce Carol Oates."

I am sure that you are an expert at self-judgment. After all, you've had enough practice, right? Who better than you to magnify your multiple flaws, faults, and weaknesses in all their glory. But, in striving to be your best, you could end up being your own worst enemy.

We all judge ourselves harshly at some point or another in life and there's nothing unusual about that. The problem arises when we do it so often that it becomes a long-lasting habit. It's one thing to kick yourself for being late to an appointment or not meeting a deadline, but if such events turn into grand general statements about your unworthiness as a whole, then that's a slippery path.

I admit that one of my old bad habits was to expect too much of myself in my working day. Not being superwoman, more

29

often than not, I found that I couldn't possibly do everything I had planned to, and this left me blaming myself for being incompetent. Now, I recognize this auto pop-up window when it appears in my thoughts and I immediately click on the small **x** button in the top right-hand corner to close it — you know the one I mean. The truth is that life is too short to reprimand myself for things I wasn't able to do in the 24 hours that I have and I try to set a more manageable work-load or list of tasks. This way, I don't go to bed feeling over-whelmed by my inadequacies or telling myself I am incompetent.

Remember from the last chapter: when we tell ourselves what we think we are like, we become that person if we are not careful.

But it's not easy to overcome all of this self-criticism that you load onto yourself day after day, week after week. Eventually, you will even become the supreme judge and jury of your imperfections, inabilities, and inadequacies, sentencing your-self to a life of discontentment and unfulfilled dreams.

You may not even be aware that you are constantly talking down to yourself, and even if you are, perhaps you feel power-less to stop it. It's a complicated type of thought pattern that many of us women experience but it is undoable if we are prepared to make some changes in our perspectives. There are many ways in which we self-criticize and judge and this chapter is about recognizing them and suggesting ways to overcome them.

Some common examples are things like blaming yourself for every negative situation or outcome. You feel personally responsible when things go wrong, even though there may have been other external factors, such as taking on the blame for the bad weather when you have planned a picnic. It could be that you are extremely hard on yourself as a whole, instead of just owning up to a one-off mistake. Failing to remember your friend's birthday does NOT make you an uncaring, selfish person. You simply forgot this event — human error. End of story!

If you are a pro at self-criticism, you will avoid taking risks in life. I don't mean refusing to go bungee jumping or skydiving, which makes perfect sense to me. I am thinking more about the times when you have refused to try something because you believe that you are going to fail. When you avoid applying for that cool job with a new tech company because you don't believe you stand a chance of getting it, that lack of action can seriously damage your future.

I know many women who find it hard to express their opinion because they are afraid of saying something stupid. Fair enough; if I find myself amongst a group of astrophysicists, I probably won't be able to add much to the conversation. But if I do the same thing when with my peers, that would be a clear sign of my judgmental self at work. I would be telling myself I have nothing worthwhile to bring to the conversation, or that I am boring, or that no one listens to me, so why bother. That's me putting myself down.

Another way in which we sell ourselves short is by constantly comparing ourselves to others. If you don't have a healthy level of self-esteem, you are vulnerable to feelings of inadequacy when meeting people more attractive, cleverer, or wealthier than you, and only feel good when you are with those you deem 'lesser' than yourself. That's a very unstable barometer of your self-worth because it is based on other people, and not on your inner balance. And guess what... there will always be someone smarter, prettier, richer than you, just as there will always be someone worse off. More often than not, you will probably end up comparing yourself with those who have more, which is going to make you feel very lacking indeed.

As women, we often have to juggle our careers with family life, which may include raising children or looking after other family members. We also want to spend time with friends, take care of our health and be good partners, daughters, mothers, sisters. It's a lot to handle and there will often be times when you feel dissatisfied with your achievements in at least one of those areas. You could end up going on and on about your shortcomings, taking them out of proportion, and being extremely hard on yourself. I know many women who do this and tell themselves that, no matter what they do, it's not enough.

Being too self-judgmental also means that you worry about possible outcomes and obsess over the oncoming disaster that you see looming on the horizon. When you aren't 100% confident in your abilities, it's easy to believe that nothing is going to work out as planned and this could even stop you from pursuing your ambitions and goals. Appearing as weak is another no-no for many women, who often struggle alone without asking for help, even though they may feel inside that they just can't cope. This is a classic self-sabotaging pattern of behavior and a mindset that can be changed.

Self-harm is something that has been associated with emotional pain that has its roots in self-criticism and can range from using toxic substances to actual self-inflicted bodily harm. It's a very complex form of behavior that really needs expert support but what I would like to stress is that it can be overcome with the right help. There is no need to suffer alone so please reach out to a professional if you are experiencing this kind of behavior.

Self-sabotage is also a common mode of behavior and has many causes, manifesting itself in various ways. It is the terrible twin of self-criticism, working behind the scenes to trip you up whenever you wish to pursue something that could bring greater joy to your life. When you put the two together, you get one big mess.

Think of self-criticism as the opposite of self-compassion and self-sabotage as the opposite of self-esteem. That's a lot of negativity that you are laying on yourself and a big lack of self-love.

Why, oh why do you do it?

First of all, I want you to chill out before you start down-talking yourself even more for being guilty of such terrible crimes. Self-criticism is not a dirty phrase. It is a perfectly normal human response to life. Being overly judgmental with yourself is one of those responses that can be explained, understood, and overcome. So, let's break down the types of negative behavior and learn what we can do to kick those habits.

When the global dieting company Weightwatchers asked 2000 women in the UK to take part in a survey in 2016 as part of its #WomanKind campaign, the results were pretty depressing. It turned out that the average woman in the study would criticize herself at least 8 times a day for similar reasons with her peers. In fact, 82% of British women involved in the study wished that they had a better relationship with themselves.

The most common self-hate slogan of the women, aged between 18 and 60, was the well-known phrase; "You're too fat." Next came, "Your hair is a mess," and "Your belly looks big." Other self-criticisms were things like; "You wish you were as photogenic as other women on social media," and "You're not wearing enough makeup."

The study also found that 42% of women admitted that they never give themselves compliments and the remaining 58% rewarded themselves with a positive comment only once a day. Over half of the women questioned said that they would often criticize themselves constantly throughout the day and that the urge to self-criticize was most intensely felt when out shopping for clothes or in front of the mirror.

I know, it sounds ludicrous, doesn't it? But it seems that these behaviors are so common that we can probably all relate to them. The rise of social media hasn't helped us to accept our appearance, with so many unreal expectations being set by a tiny minority of female influencers and celebrities. But, I have a feeling that if we couldn't blame it on social media, we would blame it on something else. A lack of self-esteem or self-worth isn't a 21st century phenomenon for women, after all. Perhaps it is simply more public now, but it has never been easy for women to assert themselves and ooze self-confidence throughout most of recorded history.

Being unkind to ourselves has definitely intensified as culture becomes more centered on how people present themselves on their social media profiles. This even exposes you to a world of criticism and makes you vulnerable to hate-talk, cyberbullying, body shaming, or worse. That's a scary thing. Personally, I don't usually upload photos of myself on any of my social media pages. It's not that I'm afraid of criticism but more that I don't feel the need to be validated in that way. This is a subject we will go into later on in the book because there are many ways to deal with the negative effects of all those platforms on our self-image and we will explore them in a separate chapter.

Going back to the survey carried out by Weightwatchers, when women were asked what qualities they wished they possessed, sentiments like 'believing in myself' and 'being more confident' came out tops. So, while outward appearance plays a large role in how women feel about themselves, they are aware of the importance of self-confidence and self-belief. I think this is an encouraging message, and all we need to do is unlearn the bad habits we have picked up that prevent us from having both.

Let's delve a little deeper into how much you personally criticize yourself. This isn't a pass or fail test but merely a chance for you to look at the aspects of your mindset that you need to change. Think about how many of the following statements you make in an average day about yourself:

1. I'm too fat/overweight

2. My hair is a mess

3. My belly looks big

4. I don't do enough exercise

5. I feel a mess next to other women

6. I'm not earning enough money

7. I'm having a 'fat day'

8. I'm wearing jeans today because I look obese

9. I wish I was as photogenic as other women on social media

10. I never believe compliments when made to me

11. I worry that people are talking about me behind my back

12. I feel underdressed

13. I'm not stylish enough

14. I don't have sex enough with my partner

15. I'm not as creative as other women

16. My butt looks huge

17. I'm not as organized as other women

18. I don't spend as much time with my friends as I should

19. I'm not wearing enough make-up

20. I'm not attractive to my partner

How many did you get? The truth is that most of us make at least one or two of these statements every day to ourselves and even one is enough to get you down. Whether you criticize your appearance, your worthiness, your attractiveness, or your lack of style, something is going on that is preventing you from feeling 100% happy.

The downside to self-criticism

Being aware of our faults and errors is a good thing if that means changing what we don't like and learning to cultivate something better. But more often than not, self-criticism is harmful because it can stunt our self-growth and lead to the following issues:

- It can prevent us from taking risks because we don't believe we will succeed
- It can stop us from being vocal about our opinions
- It makes us blame ourselves for every negative situation that occurs
- It makes us continuously compare ourselves to others
- It makes us dissatisfied with our accomplishments and demands perfection
- It impacts our mental wellbeing, often creating anxiety, depression, eating disorders, body image issues, and substance abuse

- It can provoke feelings of shame, guilt, anger, sadness, hopelessness, and worthlessness

- **The upside to self-acceptance**

WHEN YOU EMBRACE ALL OF YOUR HIGHS AND LOWS, GOOD points and bad points, strengths, and weaknesses, there is no need to be critical of yourself. You are simply who you are. This doesn't come about by fixing your hair or buying a new dress. It comes from your inner belief in yourself and your value, without a need to compare and contrast with others. Getting to that point isn't easy, but you can do it.

Look closely at the following strategies and when you have read them, choose one that you can begin to implement today. Just by starting with one, you are on your way to letting go of that asphyxiating hold self-judgment has over you.

- **Find your strengths**

TAKE A PEN AND PAPER AND NOTE DOWN YOUR STRENGTHS. It could be anything that comes to mind, such as, *I am a good friend, I am a caring mother, I am a generous person, I like to help others, I never give up, I always do the best that I can.* When you identify your strengths, read each one of them out loud at the beginning of every day. Keep them at the forefront of your mind, just like a crash helmet that will protect you from any oncoming collision. Never forget your strengths because they are part of your self-love cache.

- **Don't be so hard on yourself**

Everyone makes mistakes, believe me. When you think of a recent one that you have made, it's OK to spend some time reflecting on what you may have done wrong, but don't linger there too much. Did you fail that online job interview because you weren't prepared? That's disappointing, but there will be other opportunities for you so, until they come up, work on practicing your interview technique. In fact, put the experience under your belt and use it to grow and improve in the future.

- **Evaluate your inner criticisms**

If you constantly think that you are ugly, fat, a failure, a terrible person, and so on, press pause and look at each belief separately. Now, ask yourself, "What purpose does this thought serve in my life? Does it make me feel good about myself or not?" Once you begin to ask questions like that, I am sure that you will discover that these criticisms can go straight to the trash bin. It may seem difficult at first to let go of ingrained beliefs but you owe it to yourself to get rid of whatever isn't serving you.

- **Validate self-judgments**

Often, those negative self-judgments have been initiated by other people in your life, yet stay with you as 'truths' rather than opinions. When your mother said you were clumsy or your partner said that you complain too much, you need to ask yourself:

1. Is this a true and accurate description of me?

2. Is it true sometimes or always?

3. Could it have been true in the past but not applicable now?

If these observations are not true and accurate for you right now, yet you still allow them to judge you, then see them for what they are: unwholesome thoughts that cause pain and get in the way of self-love and self-acceptance. Shaking off hurtful words, especially by those we love, can be difficult, but remember that they are just words. No one has the right to tell you who you are and the more weight you give to their remarks, the more powerful they become.

- **Practice self-compassion**

I have mentioned self-compassion previously, and can't stress enough how important it is. Think of it as a soothing bandage to your painful wounds and allow it to heal your anxieties, fears, and doubts. Being kind to yourself should be a priority, not an exception, so begin to treat yourself as you would a dear friend and share kindness, care, and genuine concern.

- **Let go of the need for outside validation**

Much of our negative thinking also comes from how we 'think' the world sees us or how we 'think' we should be in the world. Although you will feel the need or desire to fit in, that doesn't have to be at the expense of your wellbeing. The desire to be thin, for example, may come from social pressures and that affects how badly you feel after you eat too much. The self-directed angst that follows is directly related to external influences, which is not a healthy way to be. Instead, be your own source of happiness and not reliant on the approval of others. Set your own terms of what is or isn't a healthy body weight for you and live according to your standards alone.

- **Forgive yourself**.

Self-forgiveness is truly liberating, if only you would allow yourself to do so. The act of forgiveness means letting go of self-judgment and criticism and opening up to a more joyful existence. If you can master the art of forgiveness, bitterness, pain and anger will no longer lead you to reprimand yourself for your misgivings and I highly recommend it. It does require a lot of soul-searching, especially if you have a victim mentality, so begin by repositioning your role in past events and understand the need to grow, not wither.

- **Learn to take feedback**

If you feel hurt when people give you justified or constructive feedback, this is really a reflection of your own self-criticism mechanism at work. If you can accept this kind of feedback without taking it personally, you will be doing yourself a great favor. Listen to what the other person has to say, weigh up in your mind if it is a valid point, and then use it to do better. You can't stop others from having their say, but you can deal with it differently.

- **Avoid disappointment**

When you set high expectations of yourself, it is very easy to feel that you have underachieved if you don't reach your goals. That's why you should set yourself reasonable expectations instead, based on the time, resources, and skills that you have. By all means, dream big, but don't aim for the top if you don't know how to get there, because failure will only make you feel worse about your abilities.

Now that we have explored strategies for dealing with that tendency to self-judge, it's time to tackle those self-destructive thoughts and behavior. As I said earlier, self-sabotage goes hand in hand with self-criticism, and we are going to look at ways of getting rid of that once and for all.

Don't forget to include the below affirmation in your daily life as you move forward with a sense of renewed freedom and strength!

Affirmation:

Every day is a new opportunity. I won't let self-doubt or judgment hold me back from the future.

❧ 4 ❧

STOPPING SELF-SABOTAGE

"Don't sabotage yourself. There are plenty of other people willing to do that for free."– *Jenny Lawson*

How many times have you said that you choose the totally wrong romantic partners and then complain that you are unlucky in love?

Consider how often you have stuck to a strict, calorie-controlled diet all week, only to pig out on that delicious pepperoni pizza at the weekend. Think about how often you have been going to ask your boss for a pay rise but didn't because you probably won't get it.

I think you see where I am going with this. You may WANT to do things differently, but you DON'T because you feel that you aren't worthy, good enough, capable, or any number of other reasons. Instead of pursuing your goals and dreams, you subconsciously or consciously find ways to prevent that from happening and, before you know it, have let opportunities and positive experiences pass you by. When that happens, you are the first to scorn yourself for your inability to succeed or find fulfilment and it all winds up in a familiar 'I told you so' narrative.

It does sound weird, doesn't it? But it all comes from the negative mindset that is setting you up for failure; a mindset that *thrives* on your failure. Self-sabotage and self-criticism can destroy you physically, mentally, or emotionally, throwing a spanner in your chances of happiness. How? By undermining you and putting stumbling blocks in your way as you strive to reach your goals. Self-sabotage is dangerous because it is so sneaky that you hardly even notice you are doing it, so this chapter is about recognizing it and stopping it before you self-combust.

A lot of self-sabotaging behavior has to do with fear: the kind of fear that takes over our mind even when there is no real threat. Negative thoughts like, "I'm not going to make it", can paralyze us and instead of moving on, we prefer to veer away from our goals. This is a very subtle process and you have to be aware of your inner self to catch it. Often, that perceived threat is a construct of your brain, which can't tell the difference between actual threats and perceived ones.

As I said earlier, self-sabotage can be conscious or unconscious, depending on how much self-awareness you have. One example of consciously self-sabotaging is when you go on a shopping spree, knowing full well that you will be left short of money for basics if you do so. An unconscious example could be anything that undermines your goals or values, even though you just can't see it. If you have a fear of failure, you may wait until the last minute to prepare for an upcoming exam and in doing so, unconsciously avoid achieving success. If you've been on the self-sabotage bandwagon long enough, it can leave you feeling sad, anxious, and with little drive or motivation.

Why do I self-sabotage?

The good news is that we know the reasons why people self-sabotage and have ways of pushing through that behavior to get to a healthier, more positive mindset.

- It's mostly a biological response to situations that feel threatening where avoidance seems to be a more sensible option. That says a lot about your level of self-esteem and if you aren't in a good mental place, you will try to avoid conflicts at any cost. It makes sense, and it's something we all do.
- There's a thing called 'modeling', which means that we copy behavior from childhood models and patterns. This can also include the absence of a good model, leaving us unable to react in a way that protects our self-interests. If you had an overprotective parent who worried constantly about you catching a cold, this could have made you afraid to test your limits, be adventurous or go out without feeling stressed.
- Being rejected by a parent can trigger a large dose of insecurity about personal relationships, leading you to have trust issues. This can lead you to sabotage your chances of establishing close relationships as you try to avoid further rejection.
- If you have experienced some kind of trauma in your life, you will most likely see the whole world as threatening, which you deal with by adopting self-sabotage strategies such as not traveling abroad, refusing to move house in order to secure a better job, or even neglecting your health and welfare.

It's not only women who self-sabotage, but we are very predictable in the areas that we like to practice it on. Obsessed as many of us are with weight and appearance, it's not surprising that most of our struggles in life revolve around perfecting a certain look or morphing into a particular body type. Relationships also seem to bring out the worst in our fear-factor behavior, as do our careers or jobs. Once you grasp the idea that your self-destructive behavior is attached to your lack of self-love, it will be easier for you to change it.

I've listed below some of the ways in which you may behave as you go about self-sabotaging your life. I also want you to think about what after-effects you have experienced as a result:

Finding fault in others

If you like to find fault in others, that enables you to avoid having to deal with your own issues and grow. When your partner behaves in a way that you don't like, instead of considering your part in that, you decide to break up, hence sabotaging any chances of growing from the whole experience. Sometimes no one is to blame and life just gets in the way but if you are constantly looking for excuses to disconnect, that's not going to help you build a lasting relationship of any value.

Walking away when the going gets tough

By all means, get out of a toxic situation as fast as you can but take some time first to see if you are making rash decisions based on your insecurities. Did you really make the effort to do your best in your job or was it easier to resign than to deal with an unfair boss or bitchy workmates? If you have doubts about your abilities and performance, this could lead you to give in too easily under pressure or run from conflicts or disagreements. It is easier to curl up in a ball, I admit, but that won't get you through life. We can thrive through challenges and come out the other side feeling wiser, happier, and ready to meet the next one.

Procrastination

This is a very common tactic for those of you who are dealing with self-doubt and feel overwhelmed. Here's the thing: putting something off until the last minute is a recipe for almost certain failure. But, you already know that, don't you? If you have to read up for an important meeting but decide to organize your lingerie drawer instead or get stuck on a Netflix binge, this is avoidance. You may tell yourself that you'll do it later, but what you are really saying is, "I can't cope. I don't think I can make it." As a result, you don't make it because you didn't direct your energy to the task at hand.

Dating the wrong guy

Why do you go on dates with people who you know aren't your type? If you aren't into beer-guzzling slobs who like slouching around all day, it's no surprise that your relationship ends quickly. Perhaps you are in a long-term partnership and stick it out because, although you feel unhappy, you are afraid of the alternatives. All of this is self-sabotaging your desire to be happy, but you do it anyway because you don't believe that you deserve better.

These are some main themes that run through self-sabotaging behavior and it is a good idea at this point to ask yourself: "What am I afraid of?" You can write this question down, and think about the first thing that pops into your head.

Let's say you fear that you'll never be a good mother and dig a bit deeper into why you have formed this opinion of yourself. Did something happen to you to make you believe that? Was any experience in the past linked to your thoughts about motherhood and raising children? How was your life growing up? Was it a happy childhood or did you feel unwanted or neglected? Are you worried about how it will affect your lifestyle or cause friction with your family/partner? Do you feel too young, too old, or just not sure if you can adjust? You can work around all of these issues, but you need to confront them first.

Whatever it is that you feel creates fear inside of you, lay it out and look it in the eye. Monsters under the bed don't really exist; we just believe they do until we look and see there is nothing there but our fears.

The fake you

I must mention something that is quite a buzz term recently, and that is imposter syndrome. This is basically when you believe that you aren't as competent as others think you are. Yes, you are a phony and don't deserve to be where you are and that goes for your job, your social status, your skills, and just about everything else. Funnily enough, the term was first introduced to describe high-achieving women who felt that they didn't merit having such an elevated status because... well, they were women. Now it applies to anyone who feels that they are in some way deceiving others because they know, deep inside, that they aren't worthy.

If you experience self-doubt, can't realistically assess your competence, or put your success down to external factors such as luck, then you may be suffering from imposter syndrome. You might even downplay your achievements or try to overachieve and set yourself goals that you just can't meet. All of this can lead to an anxious cycle in which you never give yourself credit for anything and can't internalize your success.

A recent independent study by Access Commercial Finance in 2019 found that, out of 3000 adults in the UK, two-thirds of the women (66%) questioned have suffered from imposter syndrome compared to over half of men (56%) within the last

12 months. Despite women working their way up the corporate ladder and starting their own businesses, it seems that many of them feel like a fake and are stressed about their peers finding out there is no Wizard of Oz after all. It could be that women experience it more frequently because they have grown up in a society that is still struggling to see them as having equal abilities as men. Despite all of the evidence to suggest the opposite, many women still feel that they, "Don't have a head for business" or "Got where they are today because of their looks". The problem grows larger if you experience it for long amounts of time because it can lead you to suffer from chronic stress-related illnesses and prevent you from enjoying your success.

I've got some practical advice that will help you to rethink your self-sabotaging behavior. As you read through each one, take a mental note of anything that rings particularly true for you. It's all about changing old habits and ways of thinking so don't expect results immediately but ease yourself into each one gradually. You will see the benefits eventually.

Stop thinking small

You may want to take up as little space as possible in the world, but that stunts your potential. Imagine what would happen if you had a big vision for yourself; something passionate you wanted to work towards and a sense of purpose. That would require you to think big and when you do that, the sky's the limit. Sit down and list your vision, your passions, and your dreams, then add your skills, talents, and qualities. It's up to you to go for whatever you want in life and there's nothing to stop you but your small thinking.

Worry less

Worry sucks all the energy out of you. It handicaps your efforts, drains you of positivity, and leaves you feeling overwhelmed. Self-sabotage at its finest! One way to deal with this is to think of constructive actions rather than destructive ones. If you are losing sleep over financial problems, they aren't going to go away with insomnia. Instead, draw up a strategy for dealing with them, seek the help of a friend or expert, work out ways of improving your situation and be proactive. You may not solve all of your issues in a day, but you will definitely sleep better at night.

Give yourself a break

So you're having a bad day. That is only one in thousands and instead of giving it more importance than it deserves, put it into perspective. You are the whole package, with strengths and weaknesses, not defined by one bad day, or any other day. Remember your past accomplishments and how you overcame challenges to get where you are now and honor them. Accept a compliment... why not! Spend some time indulging yourself; take a long hot bath, treat yourself to a meal out, or whatever it is that brings pleasure to your day. Just because one thing went wrong, that doesn't mean you have to suffer and wallow in self-pity.

Be honest

It's very tempting to want to please other people all the time because this makes us feel wanted, loved, and appreciated. But when that goes against what you really want to do, you become a doormat. It is perfectly OK to say 'no' when others expect you to say 'yes'. The next time your friend asks you to pick her up from the train station while you have arranged to stay home and chill out, simply tell her that although you would love to, you have made other plans. Your 'no' is important because it honors your self-esteem so use it more often, no guilt attached.

Assert yourself

There's an urban myth that successful women are pushy and bossy. Those characteristics alone are enough to make anyone stay out of the spotlight, even when they should be in it. You have skills, talents, and achievements, so don't be ashamed to show them off. If that means taking a stand, stepping up, or speaking out, do it. Have your own back and approach obstacles with confidence, safe in the knowledge that you know what you are talking about. That's not pushy, that's called being assertive, and the more you do it, the more empowered you will feel.

Liberate your desires

You should seriously ask yourself what you want, personally, professionally, sexually, and get in touch with your deepest desires. Keeping them locked up is like buying a snazzy new dress and never wearing it because you don't want to attract attention to yourself. That dress is going to sit gathering dust in your wardrobe, just like your desires, which are all a healthy part of who you are. Embrace them, express them and go for them, without feeling the need to justify them. If you don't, you will continue to feel stifled and stuck, and you deserve so much more in life.

Spend more time with those you love

No doubt you are a one-woman wonder, but sharing your trials and tribulations with trusted peers, friends or family will bring much more balance into your life. Everyone needs support at times and that can be psychological, emotional, or professional. Trying to do it all alone and self-isolating is a safe way to go about things, because it protects you, or so you think. In reality, it's your self-sabotaging habit that has convinced you you don't need help, even when you are struggling. Reach out, hang out and chill out with your women friends — you all need each other.

Don't sabotage others

There's nothing worse than putting other women down and if you are guilty of that, think about what that says about your own insecurities. Just because you have had to work hard to get where you are in life, doesn't mean that you should sabotage the efforts of others to reach the same level of success as you. Being condescending or patronizing won't earn you any Brownie points and certainly won't make you respected or loved. If you have had it hard, remember that, and give a helping hand to others whenever you can. That's a truly empowering way to live life.

Spot your triggers

Learn how to recognize those self-sabotaging habits by paying attention to what is triggering them. Think about what is making you feel stressed out, forcing you to behave in a self-destructive manner. It could be things like the angry tone of your partner, which makes you shut down even if the anger isn't directed at you. You may be bored and your mind begins to wander (always a risk of recycling toxic thoughts when that happens), or you could be in a state of fear. Self-doubt may raise its head when you are under stress and even if things are going well, you could experience imposter syndrome.

What I would suggest as good practice to help you overcome your self-sabotaging is to keep a daily journal. It can make a big difference when you put your thoughts and feelings down on paper. Not only is it a cleansing process, during which you unload all of your fears and doubts, but you will be amazed at how much clarity you can get from it. I used to keep a diary when I was very young, which acted as a confidante of sorts. Whenever I re-read what I had written, it helped me to see where I had been over-reacting and where I had been justified. It provided an emotional compass for me during my teenage years and then I abandoned the habit for a long time.

After being fully absorbed in my business and providing self-empowerment seminars to women, it suddenly dawned on me one day that I wasn't practicing what I had been preaching, so I began a daily journal again. As a result, I rediscovered the benefits of getting it all out of my head and down on paper. It helps me to reflect, assess and affirm what I am doing and what my goals are. It is my best friend once again and we can always use an extra friend, right?

In the next chapter, we are going to take a look at the BIG issue of body and self-image. I know that this is a subject many of you are concerned about and one that is preventing you from truly loving yourself. I want you to leave your negative mindset at the door as you enter the next chapter.

Take a seat, get comfy and get ready to fall in love with your body again.

Affirmation

I remind myself of my values daily and will not place roadblocks in their way.

LOVE YOUR BODY

"You can't hate yourself happy. You can't criticize yourself thin. You can't shame yourself worthy. Real change begins with self-love and self-care."
— *Jessica Ortner*

At last! This year, I can go on that long-awaited beach vacation safe in the knowledge that my excess pounds are normal. Yes, you heard me. I'm normal!

And how do I know this? Because some very big high street fashion brands have started featuring fuller-figured women in their swimsuit campaigns this season. That was a long time coming, but thankfully, we are now seeing women with all body types and sizes in swimwear being portrayed as attractive, sexy, and most of all, acceptable, in the mainstream media. It seems that you don't need to have the body of a prepubescent 14-year-old anymore to wear a fashionable bikini and it is OK to flaunt your curves and still feel good.

So, how long is it going to take you to accept **your** body?

You probably have a love-hate relationship with it, or at least, parts of it. Thighs too big? Butt too small? Chest not full enough? Stomach fat a pain? Too skinny in general? Most women obsess over some aspects of their body, cutting them up into different sections as if they were joints of meat. You probably feel that you have some good features and some bad, but believe that if only you had the perfect legs, stomach, or butt, that your life would be so much better. This is an interesting myth that many women of all ages have bought into and we'll take a look at why it is so misleading a bit later. Men also suffer from negative body image issues and can experience many of the problems that women go through such as body shaming and eating disorders, but this is a book about women and the obstacles they face.

A lot of women may also despise their weight as a whole and are totally dedicated to changing it. They desire to be thinner, fuller, firmer, fitter, taller, shorter, or even younger-looking, and will go to great lengths to try to achieve that. Quirky diet fads, exhausting miracle workouts, weird weight-reducing products, and costly cosmetic surgery are just some of the lengths to which women will go to fight the fat wars. Forget about working on your inner confidence and self-esteem: you have to have a fabulous body to be happy, right? This is the kind of narrative that we are engaged in, both with ourselves and within society as a whole, and it's an endless struggle.

I think it's time to raise the white flag and make peace with who you are.

That doesn't mean eating unhealthily, missing out on exercise, or neglecting to take care of yourself. All of those are important for your physical and emotional health, wellbeing, and self-confidence. But if you can remove the need to be something you are not (and may never be) from the equation, you can get to a much happier place without all of the stress.

Here are ten interesting facts about body image and how it affects women, who take many of their cues from family, friends, social pressure, and the media.

1. Approximately 91% of women in the US are unhappy with their bodies and try dieting to achieve their ideal body shape. Despite this, only 5% of women naturally possess the ideal body type portrayed by American media.
2. Those who are unhappy with their bodies and don't eat healthily may develop eating disorders later on such as fasting, constant dieting, binging, or purging.
3. More than 1/3 of those admitting to 'normal dieting' will develop pathological dieting, with a quarter of those people eventually suffering from a partial or full eating disorder.
4. Self-esteem and body image go hand in hand, with adolescents developing eating disorders, experiencing suicidal thoughts, and engaging in sexual activity way too early.
5. A huge 95% of people with eating disorders are between the ages of 12 and 25.
6. The same source as above found that around 58% of college-aged girls feel pressured to be a certain weight.
7. Reality TV greatly influences how young girls feel about their bodies, and the more they watch, the more likely they are to dwell on their appearance.
8. Women students who consume more mainstream media than others place greater importance on sexiness and overall appearance than they do on abilities.
9. A survey conducted on how many people would consider cosmetic surgery in the future showed that more than 40% of women and about 20% of men

thought it to be an option. Few differences were
noted across age, marital status, and race.

10. Sadly, out of all those suffering from an eating
disorder, only about 10% will seek professional help.

The above figures come from various studies that took place in the United States in 2014, and we can get a good idea of how important body image is, but also how destructive it can be if left to spiral out of control. Recent figures from across the pond in the UK carried out by the Mental Health Foundation in March 2019 found that one in 5 adults (20% of those involved in the survey) felt shame about their body image, over one third (34%) felt down or low, and 19% even felt disgusted by it!

Sadly, 37% of teenagers felt upset, 31% felt ashamed, and 34% of adults said they felt anxious or depressed because of their body image.

In addition, 13% of adults experienced suicidal thoughts stemming from hang-ups about their body image, 21% said advertising images increased their stress and 40% of teenagers blamed social media for their body image issues.

We seem to be living in a world where the way we look is having a massive impact on our well-being, which is a shocking realization. Why can't we just be happy with ourselves and accept our bodies? What is causing us so much stress, anxiety, and heartache in the first place? If we can get to the bottom of that, it is possible to break free from these negative impulses to be something that we are not and to love ourselves, nonetheless.

Today, girls grow up receiving messages about how they look, and this carries on into adulthood. A girl's appearance is more likely to be praised than her achievements or actions and that makes her think that her looks are more important than who she is inside. The media loves to focus on thin, attractive, young women, manipulating images with sophisticated technology to make them look even more perfect. As a result, this has become the beauty benchmark and one that most girls and women are trying to reach.

But it's not all the media's fault. Some past events in your life may have caused you to develop a negative body image, such as:

- Being bullied or teased at school about your looks, or even by parents, family, or friends.
- Being criticized for your appearance and told you're too fat, too thin, or ugly.
- Being underweight, overweight, or obese.
- There are also rare cases of people having a distorted body view and this is a serious medical condition.

In a thin world, being overweight has, until recently, been frowned upon by the society that we live in. Those women who are obese are much more likely to be dissatisfied with their bodies and low self-esteem doesn't help. There are exceptions to this, of course, and not every woman is hard on themselves because of their weight. I recall one day in a new yoga class I had joined meeting Sofia — a woman in her late 30s who seemed quite overweight by my standards. I wondered how on earth she would be able to do all of the graceful moves yet, to my surprise, she was the most flexible, supple person I have ever met. Her extra pounds were no barrier to the way she executed beautiful, fluid sun salutations, while I couldn't even manage the down dog position without falling flat on my face.

I was surprised at my own level of discrimination against Sofia, and all the Sofias in this world, which got me thinking that my perception of women carrying extra weight was also incredibly biased. But weight doesn't have to be an issue that determines body image. If you have high self-esteem, feel comfortable in your skin, and aren't influenced by external forces such as social media, you can love yourself no matter what.

I don't need to tell you how you feel about your body. What I do need to remind you of is that your body is unique and beautiful in its own way.

I know you may find that hard to believe, but until you do so, you will always be seeking perfection in a world that is constantly changing the goalposts about what is classed as beautiful, attractive, and acceptable. Apart from that fact, it simply does you more harm than good to be overly-concerned with your appearance at the expense of your inner well-being. Nurturing self-love for your body, with all of its pros and cons is the first step to feeling fully alive, content, and happy. And it's not some distant goal that you need to chase — it's within you already.

Reversing that negative body image

There are many ways that you can do this, and a lot of it begins with changing some of your habits, as well as taking the time to nurture your inner self. You can go through this process slowly as you try to unlearn patterns of thoughts and emotions that may have been with you for years and years. Take it easy and avoid being hard on yourself as you begin to understand how to feel more content with your body.

- You can begin by thinking about the way you identify yourself when you look in the mirror. Noticing your imperfections is a habit that does you no good at all, and they are reinforced by your old friend, that negative inner critic. How easy is it for you to look in the mirror just once a day and feel totally satisfied with what you see? To be honest, I think it's a great idea to have as few mirrors as possible around the house. This will help you to stop being infatuated with how you look from morning to night. It's not about denial, but more to do with shifting your priorities.

- The language you use to describe yourself is also important and the feedback you may get from others could reinforce how good or bad you are feeling even more. Don't keep asking if you look fat in these jeans, this top, or that dress. If you want to wear any of them, do so without asking about how you look. Do you enjoy those jeans? Then wear them. It's as simple as that. You've also got to walk the talk, so if someone makes a negative comment about how you are dressed, such as, "That skirt makes you look obese," be prepared to express how comfortable, sexy, and attractive you feel in it, end of story.

Getting away from that negative self-image isn't going to be easy. After all, we are inundated daily with model-like girls who seem to look absolutely fabulous, no matter what they wear. Clothing is a big problem for women who feel their body type doesn't match 'the norm' and shopping for clothes can be a major trigger point for anxiety.

- How about, rather than popping into trendy 'teen' stores' when you are not a size 6 or 8, which will only lead to tears, you try real women's shops that cater for all sizes and body types? Also, I suggest that you go clothes shopping without taking a friend along because you could easily be influenced by their choices. How many times have you been talked out of buying something you really liked because a friend commented that it's too low-cut, too long, too short, too tight, or too revealing? Learn to know what suits you, compliments you, and flatters, without the need for a second opinion.

As women, we have a curious relationship with our bodies. On the one hand, we are completely connected with our reproductive system and our monthly menstrual cycle, yet we are often completely disconnected from the value that our body has. We ignore all of the amazing things it can do such as running, dancing, breathing, dreaming, and treat it more like a broken down car that needs new parts every now and again, or a battering in the body shop to knock the chassis into shape.

- It will help if you can get more in touch with your body, which you can do by taking part in activities that you enjoy, such as working out, swimming, cycling, boxing, or whatever it is that feels right for you.
- Be in awe of your female form — men have been doing just that since time began! Femininity is inherent in all women by definition, and nurturing your feminine side will definitely allow you to be kinder to yourself. You can do this by exploring different ways of dressing, changing your hairstyle, or fixing your makeup. Instead of keeping that new dress or necklace for a special occasion, wear them today and celebrate life now, without waiting for the future.
- Get to know your body better. Notice how it reacts to the way you are feeling. When you are stressed, your shoulders hunch up and when you feel down, you hang your head low. You may also experience aches and pains that are related to your emotional frame of mind and should keep an eye on these.

- Take up an activity that requires a lot of body control, such as ballet or weightlifting, and gain an appreciation of how wonderful your body is. You will learn that your body is truly an amazing thing.
- Make a list of the ten things that you like about yourself — anything that isn't linked to your appearance. What about things like having a great sense of humor, being a fantastic football player, or a great boss? I am sure that you can think of many more.

Going back to my friend Sofia, she wasn't just a yoga teacher's dream. She was also very sexy — something about the way she held herself and how she walked. She simply exuded self-confidence, which also made her incredibly attractive to men. For her, the extra weight she was carrying wasn't a burden — it was a bonus! (Still working on my down dog...).

There has been a myriad of influential women in the past who have helped to define what is or isn't a desirable body type. Marilyn Monroe always springs to mind because of her curvaceous body that became such a symbol of sexuality. Every woman in the 1940s and 50s wanted to look just like her. Then we began to idolize the childlike figure of Twiggy in the 60s — fat was no longer fun — and being skinny was in.

As the supermodel era emerged in the 70s and 80s, the emphasis was on looking healthy, sporty, and full of fun, only to be rejected in the 90s when models like Kate Moss rose to stardom. Back to being wafer-thin again, women and young girls, in particular, began wanting to shed those pounds in order to mirror the body image of an adolescent. A very famous celebrity, known for her part in a family TV reality show has, in many ways, challenged again the ideal of what is or isn't the body beautiful, emphasizing her large derriere as part of her sex appeal. Whether you love it or hate it, the fact is that there has been a sharp demand for plastic surgeons to carry out butt implants as women rush to boost their 'assets'.

Of course, this is just another passing trend. It is also one more example of how we tend to compartmentalize our bodies or see them as imperfect and therefore undesirable. And one question I do want to ask you is this: who are you trying to impress? Your fans, your followers, your friends, your boyfriend, husband, lover?

When you consider the motivation behind any kind of invasive surgery to enhance a certain aspect of your appearance, make sure that you are doing it for you, and not for others.

The social media trap

We have to get back to embracing our complete body form, no matter what that may be. You won't be able to do that if you continue to spend countless hours of your day on social media, following women who have been airbrushed, nipped, tucked, and digitally filtered.

All the research that has been carried out so far about the effects of social media has shown how negatively it can impact our self-esteem, so I have some tips to help you get out of that toxic cycle:

- Reduce the amount of time that you spend on social media each day. Bombarding yourself with images of women who seem more beautiful than you can seriously damage your sense of self-esteem and the more you do it, the more you compound the effect. Live your own life instead of watching others live theirs.
- Be selective about who you follow. Instead of scrolling through the feed of super-shiny celebrities and picture-perfect influencers, choose to follow

women who are successful despite their appearance. By taking control of what you expose yourself to, you will be creating your own filter and allowing yourself to be influenced by positive role models.

- Unfollow or unfriend anyone who may lead you to feel dissatisfied with your own body image — you don't need that in your life.
- If you can't keep off social media, follow people who have similar bodies to your own. There are plenty of positive groups and personalities out there, proudly celebrating their body type, as well as their particular ethnic or social background. Join them and celebrate your own body too!
- Even though you know that much of what you see on social media is fake, your brain still wants to believe it, so it's important to keep reminding yourself that most of it is simply an illusion. By all means, follow your favorite personality, but don't forget that they don't look perfect 24/7, because that is just impossible.
- This one is going to hurt: the next time you upload a selfie, don't edit it first. Put yourself out there as you are, and help other women to be brave enough to do that too. You do know that retouching your image is a bit like cheating right? It's not the real you, so focus on loving yourself as you are — that is an extremely powerful step to take and one which you won't regret.
- Being perfect is too much hard work. Concentrate on being a better person, one who will inspire others to raise their confidence levels, and be part of a global shift towards all-embracing self-love.
- Don't be a part of the body-shaming culture. Offering unsolicited advice to friends about what they eat or how they look is not only rude but can

have a powerful negative impact on their self-esteem. Guilt is a heavy load to bear, so don't be responsible for passing that onto anyone, including yourself.

Thankfully, more celebrities are now talking about body shaming and are trying to raise awareness of the issue and promote body positivity. Women like Serena Williams and Kelly Clarkson are taking a stance against this cruel phenomenon that we see all around us, and you can also play an active role in getting rid of it once and for all. Creating a positive body image depends on you accepting your own imperfections which, ultimately, will stop you from placing unfair judgments on others.

It's great to look and feel your best in whatever skin you are in. By investing in yourself, you nurture an inner beauty that will shine through to all those around you. When you spend less time on your smartphone, you can devote more time to doing things that you love, and that's one of the secrets to real happiness.

Finally, if you want to change your body weight, do it with the help of a trained professional. Crash diets and quick fixes don't work. You need to change your mindset and lifestyle; something that is much easier to achieve if you don't feel that you are doing it alone. Join a weight loss program if you want to shed some pounds, which will also help you to set realistic goals and adopt healthier eating habits.

If you have a negative body image due to being underweight, work with a doctor or specialist to gain weight healthily and take care of any underlying health problems you may have. Joining a support group can also be extremely useful as you will find yourself amongst other women who understand your problem and can help you to reach your targets.

Practice makes perfect, so the more posit[...] have about your self-image, the fewer negative [...] crop up in your mind. While most of us have som[...] about our appearance, we have learned to live with th[...] the truth is, they make us unique. So what if your calves [...] too thick or your hips are too narrow? This is your genetic makeup and part of who you are, so embrace it instead of despising it.

As we get older, our focus tends to be less about our body parts and more about enjoying inner peace, so why not start practicing that now? You are never too young to begin loving yourself!

In the next chapter, we will be talking about some of the reasons why you may have such low self-esteem, and I am going to give you some strategies to help you overcome that, using the language of love.

Let's end with this wonderfully inspiring affirmation, which perfectly sums up everything that I have been talking about in this chapter. Repeat this five times a day — before every meal — and say it from the heart, which is where self-love is found.

Affirmation:

Body, if you can love me for who I am, I promise to love you for who you are.

ITIZING YOU

*"Put yourself at the top of your to-do list every single day
and the rest will fall into place."*
— *Unknown.*

What's on your to-do list today, and how much of that revolves around other people?

The chances are, that your day is filled with obligations such as work and family commitments, with little free time to focus on anything else. Whether you do the 9 to 5 work-commute routine, work from home, or are a full-time parent/carer, you probably often feel pulled in a lot of different directions.

It may be the demands of your boss, the expectations of your friends, or the needs of your family that keep you busy from morning till night, and this may all seem perfectly acceptable to you. It could become so normal that you don't even realize that while you are running around after everyone else, you are neglecting your own needs. You may find it difficult to say no when asked to help out, or haven't set reasonable boundaries that can give you space to live your life too.

Many women feel obliged to take on the role of carer, are more than ready to compromise when it comes to their personal desires, and think nothing of putting others first. My sister-in-law is a great example of this and the more I notice this about her, the more I see the wear and tear that it has on her personal well-being. Dina is a lovely person; caring, compassionate, kind, and a great mother, who will go out of her way to tend to everyone's needs.

As a primary school teacher, she spends her working day with young children and always goes to visit her elderly mother after finishing work. She'll do the tidying up, see to medications, and keep her mother company for a couple of hours, despite having a paid, live-in carer for her mother. When Dina returns home, she sees to her own household chores and cooks for her husband (who, incidentally, works from home) and two grown-up sons. I think she probably collapses into bed around 10 pm, feeling exhausted and drained.

I do admire her values of wanting to be a good daughter, wife, and mother, but see that she devotes no time at all to herself. As a consequence, she has told me that she feels desperately unhappy and trapped, yet can't seem to find a way to break the cycle of prioritizing the needs of others before her own. The obligation that she feels to put others first is such a strong pattern of behavior that she can't get past it. There are millions of Dinas out there; women who have become accustomed to making their happiness a low priority, women who are so selfless that they become empty and deeply discontent.

If you are single, you may not have that many commitments, but still spend a large part of your day making sure that you are pleasing people, be that your colleagues, your boss, friends, or even neighbors. There's nothing wrong with that, unless you give so much of your time and effort that there's nothing left for you. Those of you with families will know that from the moment you become a parent, you automatically focus on seeing to the needs of your children and put your own priorities on the back burner. Nothing wrong with that, until you completely run out of steam and become of no use to anyone.

If you are a stay-at-home-mum, not only will you be involved in rearing your children, but you probably wear a few other hats as well. You may be the cleaner, cook, plumber, electrician, technician, accountant, teacher, playmate, counselor, psychologist, and supervisor. That's a lot to take on in a day, leaving very little room to simply being you and meeting your needs. Perhaps you are in part-time or full-time employment, and still need to spend your free time in any or all of the above roles, which can be extremely demanding and stressful.

We've kind of gotten used to this idea that prioritizing ourselves is selfish and that we aren't good mothers, wives, partners, daughters, or friends if we self-indulge. Our job is to care, nurture, love, and protect our family, which means attending to all of their needs. You could even say that we aren't supposed to have any needs of our own when fulfilling that role, which is why many women suffer from a midlife identity crisis once their children reach adulthood. They suddenly realize that they don't know what their role is anymore, since their 'job' has been to look after dependents for the past 20 years, so now what?

Making yourself a priority in life isn't selfish. It's an absolute necessity.

I know that's something you may find difficult to get your head around because it goes against everything that you have probably been taught until now. We women are brought up to be professional givers and expert multi-taskers who selflessly strive to make everyone happy, even at the expense of our own needs. It's no coincidence that we feel guilty when we want to take some 'me' time or choose to focus on ourselves instead of others. Family and friends may find it hard to accept that you need to look after yourself first and society often frowns upon women who don't seem to be sticking to the rules in that respect.

But prioritizing yourself doesn't mean ignoring the needs of others, having a 'couldn't care less' attitude, or being neglectful. It simply means making sure that you are taking enough care of yourself so that you are in good physical and emotional health. It's not an either-or dilemma. You can still be caring, nurturing, compassionate and helpful while seeing to your own wants and desires. In fact, it's a must. Look at it this way: how efficient can you really be if you are running on empty?

It's admirable to be altruistic and to want to help others because that ultimately makes us feel good too. Knowing that you have done your best to tend to a sick relative, helped out a friend, or gone out of your way to assist a colleague are all marvelous acts and no one would deny that. But often, there is a cost, which may include forsaking your free time, changing your plans, or having to offer too much emotional support. You may push yourself to the limits, forgo your own wants and even make sacrifices that can have a negative impact on your life. If you aren't aware that this is going on, not only will the wear and tear eventually show in your health and well-being, but it will also have a ripple effect on the ones you are trying to take care of in the first place.

When you see it from that perspective, self-prioritizing is really about maintaining a certain regard for yourself that enables you to be your best. Self-compassion is fundamental to that, and if you want to create a good life for yourself and those who matter to you the most, you need to practice it daily. Even a boxer in a ring needs to spend some time out in the corner to have his injuries seen to, right?

Research on how health workers are affected by their jobs point to two outcomes — burnout and compassion fatigue. This is an example of how working in the caring profession can cause serious problems to those involved, but it also shows that when you are constantly seeing to the physical, emotional, or practical needs of others, eventually it will wear you down. You could suffer from stress, a feeling of hopelessness, indifference, pessimism, and a lack of energy and motivation. If that was your full-time job, you would probably be granted sick leave in order to get better, but when it's your life, how can you take time off from that?

As I said earlier, we women have grown up thinking that we have to give it our all and it wasn't until very recently that we heard it's OK to have needs, desires or demands. Even expressing those three is often hard for us though, because we don't want any fingers pointing at us or be accused of complaining. No, we prefer to soldier on, paying little attention to what we want, because it's not a priority.

I'd like you to look at the examples below, and decide how comfortable or uncomfortable you would be in each situation, on a scale of 1 to 5 (1 being perfectly OK with it and 5 being totally uncomfortable). Here goes:

1. You and your partner have been invited to a party but they become sick. You go to the party anyway.
2. Your kids are begging you to get a dog but you refuse to give in to them.
3. You spend all day Saturday shopping with friends, even though your boyfriend wanted to spend the day with you at home.

4. You arrange tennis lessons for every Sunday morning, leaving your partner to look after the kids and cook lunch.
5. Your best friend wants to borrow your new dress but you refuse to lend it to her.
6. You make the decision not to have children, even though your parents were so looking forward to being grandparents.
7. You arrange to pay for a caregiver to attend to your elderly father's daily needs, rather than providing the care yourself.
8. You ask a neighbor to pick up your kids from school today, as you have a hair and nail appointment.
9. You refuse to work overtime this Friday, much to your boss's dismay, because you have made plans to go to the cinema with friends.
10. You decide to have a short mini-break alone this weekend, without your partner.

I can already tell that you may find some of the above pretty uncomfortable proposals and a few of them may even be completely unthinkable. I also know why you would feel that way. How dare you choose yourself over others? That's shameful, selfish, and downright uncaring. How could you!

Yes, this is the kind of criticism that you may believe you will hear, and no one likes to be criticized. In fact, most of us can't imagine anything worse than being called selfish, because it goes against everything that we aspire to be. And that's exactly why we don't prioritize ourselves — we don't want to be bad people.

The idea that women are natural carers and nurturers is deeply ingrained in many societies and, traditionally, that is the role they have been given. The expectation was that women can offer their services from morning till night without needing any care in return and it's a concept that has been handed down from one generation to the next. Many of us are learning to overcome this mindset as we forge our own paths in our professional and family lives but there is still some hesitancy when it comes to challenging this role of full-time carer. It's almost as if we feel that we are betraying the ones we love, and in doing so, we betray ourselves instead.

But, hold on a minute. Didn't we say that taking care of your own needs is important? That means doing what is best for you so you can ultimately be your best for others.

- If your partner is sick with something like a common cold, what point is there in you staying home? Why would you feel guilty about going to the party without them?
- No matter how much you love dogs, you know more than anyone the amount of time and attention they need. If your kids aren't old enough to handle that responsibility, what's so wrong with refusing their wishes?
- You love having an all-girls shopping day out, and would much prefer that instead of spending all day at home. Is that so bad?
- As for those tennis lessons, don't you deserve some time off from your domestic and parenting duties once a week?
- Regarding that new dress, you haven't even worn it yet so refusing to lend it out seems perfectly reasonable, doesn't it?
- Your life choices are yours alone, and although it may go against your parent's desires when you decide not to have children, you have to stay true to your values, don't you?
- The strain of having to look after your elderly father

may just be too much for you to handle. It's fine to pass on that responsibility to someone else who is also a professional, isn't it?

- Asking for help with your kids when you need it isn't such a bad thing, and wanting to look your best doesn't make you selfish or vain, right?
- Valuing your free time, even if your boss doesn't, is very important and you don't need to feel that you have let him down by refusing to work overtime, do you?
- Spending any time alone can be just what you need to recharge and we could all do with more of that, so why would the idea of going on a mini-break alone present such a problem?

Maybe you would feel OK about doing some of the above, or perhaps you believe that several of them are just darn wrong. Whatever your beliefs are, I'm not trying to change them or to challenge your values. What I would like to do is ask you to consider what aspects of your life may be draining you or harming your well-being. Can you do that?

Often, many of the problems we are trying to cope with have to do with that running on empty syndrome. Giving too much of our time and energy to others can leave us feeling drained, tired, frustrated, and discontent. Part of that is because we haven't learned to say 'no', but mostly it's about our misconceptions surrounding what we should or shouldn't be doing. There are several reasons for that, and like most things, a lot of them stem from how we were brought up and what expectations have been placed on us. But, as you know, we can change and it's never too late to do a mental reboot and view life differently.

Drawing the line

How easy is it to draw the line between acting selfishly and living a life that brings you contentment and happiness? How do you balance looking after yourself with being a good partner, friend, mother, or colleague? You may feel confused about that, or the line seems blurry, which means that you find it difficult to self-prioritize. Below are a few questions that you may want to ask yourself to help you to gain clarity:

1 Do you feel depleted, exhausted?

2 How energetic do you feel and how often do you do things that you enjoy?

3 How often do you think that you 'should' help someone else, even though you don't feel like it?

4 How often do you go through the motions of helping although not fully engaging in a meaningful way?

5 How often do you feel recharged by what you do?

6 How often do you take a break from your responsibilities?

7 How often do you go above and beyond to satisfy the needs of others?

And here are some more to think about:

8 Do you want to be the perfect mother, chef, chauffeur, coach, cleaner, lover, partner?

9 Do you feel that you have made personal sacrifices in order to make others content?

10 Do you complain a lot about not being happy?

11 Do you feel guilty when you don't give 100% of your time and energy to others?

12 Do you occasionally have stress-related outbursts?

All of the above are normal habits of many women; learned ways of behaving, thinking, and feeling that we have adopted along the way and, like all habits, they can be broken. It's a wonderful thing to be kind, generous, and caring, but when we lose touch with our own desires, wants, and needs, there is a fallout and our quality of life is affected. In that respect, it's good to be 'selfish' now and again, if that means putting yourself first so you are better able to help others. That's the concept that you have to get your head around, and once you understand that self-care and self-compassion can make you happier, you will be able to enjoy life more with your loved ones.

They say that charity begins at home and, in this case, so does self-love. With some small changes to your daily routine, you can begin to see the benefits of tending more to your needs and prioritizing yourself. Start introducing the tips below into your life gradually and note how you feel after a few weeks. As you begin to adopt new habits, you will feel a renewed sense of energy and contentment, while still being the caring, loving woman that everyone knows you are.

- **Make time for yourself**

Whether it's ten minutes a day, an hour, or longer, get used to dedicating some time to yourself on a daily basis. Rather than slowing you down from all the things you have to do, this will enable you to feel stronger. In that time, do something that helps you to focus on yourself, be it walking, meditation, or writing in your journal. Anything that nourishes your inner you is fine.

- **Give yourself a pat on the back**

When you acknowledge your achievements, you will feel a greater sense of joy and pride. Whatever tasks you have completed, tell yourself 'well done' because you handle a lot and deserve praise for that. There's no need to dwell on what you haven't done as that will only make you feel discontented and disappointed in yourself.

- **Create SMART personal tasks**

Set yourself three personal tasks that you want to do each day and make sure that they are specific, manageable, achievable, realistic, and time-bound. If three seems like too many, reduce that number to two. They should be things that add to your self-care such as a five-minute workout, a facial, reading a chapter of a book, going for a short walk. Anything that is done for pure pleasure is worth doing often!

- **Eat for happiness**

The food you eat turns into energy, so choose wisely when you go to the supermarket. Avoid buying over-processed, fatty foods with artificial preservatives, no matter how difficult that may be. Fill your cart with fresh produce and begin eating more healthily, which is a great way to spoil yourself and boost your immune system.

- **Stop trying to multitask**

The only one who truly appreciates your multitasking skills is you, and at great cost to your stress levels. Instead of trying to do everything simultaneously, focus on doing one thing at a time. No one expects you to be perfect so stop telling yourself that they do and remember to add your SMART tasks to your day — they are equally important.

- **Sleep soundly**

After running around all day tending to the needs of others, you may find that stress prevents you from having a good night's sleep when you finally go to bed. You need to adopt a sleeping routine that works to your advantage and this includes no screen time for at least one hour before bed, not eating heavy meals late at night, or consuming stimulants such as tea or coffee. Aim to get 7-8 hour's sleep and you can even have a lie-in at weekends — you are allowed!

- **Spoil yourself**

Believe me, it is perfectly fine to indulge yourself now and again and it doesn't have to be anything extravagant. Treating yourself to something simple can boost your mood and it's a way of honoring yourself. You can pick up a few flowers on your way home or sit down to your favorite dessert. Whatever it is, know that you deserve some small pleasure in life without feeling guilty about it.

The above examples are easy habits that you can start introducing to your life and they won't disrupt your daily responsibilities. But making yourself a priority isn't just about easy hacks. It also requires you to have a conversation with yourself about what is important to you, what problems you are facing and finding ways to alter your perspectives.

Here is where writing down how you feel can really help. You could invest in a journal, which is a great way to express yourself and it also gives you the chance to chart your progress over time. Any old notebook will do but why not buy yourself a fancy one and enjoy writing in it even more? Go on, treat yourself.

You can begin by making a list of what makes you happy. It could be spending time with friends, walking along the beach, traveling, going to concerts, staying home and watching movies, or even mountain biking. Just write down whatever comes into your head and after that, consider how often you do those things.

Next, write down how you feel when doing any of these activities. Do you feel free, content, excited, relaxed, pumped? These are all positive vibes that can release stress and more than that; these are all feelings that you need to experience in life. They bring wholeness and richness to your very being and help you to nurture more self-esteem and inner balance. It can't all be about meeting the demands, needs, and wants of others at the expense of your own well-being. Let's face it; if you feel better about yourself, you will project that to others around you too.

Another thing that you can include in your journal is a list of some of the occasions when you have said yes to someone when you would much rather have said no. As you write them down, think about how you felt when you agreed to them. It's a common habit, as we don't wish to disappoint, let down, or come across as mean. You may, for example, have canceled a night at the theater because your friend just broke up with her boyfriend and wanted a shoulder to cry on. It could be that you had agreed to order pizza because your partner fancied it when you would have much rather preferred to eat Chinese. No big deal, you may say, but if you make a habit of being a 'yes' person all the time, you are actually saying 'no' to your own desires or wants.

This is something I have already mentioned earlier in the book, but it really is OK to say 'no' sometimes. You will thank yourself for it and, in reality, you are showing others that you too have needs that should be met. There is nothing wrong with that. It doesn't make you mean, selfish, uncaring, neglectful, inconsiderate, self-centered, egotistical, thoughtless, insensitive, or uncharitable. It makes you human.

I think that, deep down inside, you know that you need to value yourself more. You need to make yourself a priority, and you need to introduce and maintain boundaries. You are a caring person, so please begin with yourself. You can be big-hearted, generous, and kind whilst protecting your own needs. If people are draining your energy or disregarding your boundaries, you need to think about how to reset that balance for your own sake.

Free up more time for yourself, honor your own needs more often, encourage others to begin treating you with more respect, ask for help when you feel overwhelmed, and love yourself more. As for setting boundaries, that's something we are going to delve into in the next chapter so, until then, take care of yourself — you deserve it!

Affirmation:

When I pour into myself, I can shine my light onto others.

❧ 7 ❧

MASTERING YOUR
RELATIONSHIPS

*"The relationship we have with ourselves sets the foundation for
every other relationship we have."*
— *Gina Senarighi*

How many relationships do you have in your life and how well do you manage them?

From the moment we are born, we enter into relationships. It begins with our mother, father, siblings, grandparents, aunts, uncles, nephews & nieces, carers, or nannies. By the time we reach adulthood, we can add friends, partners, lovers, colleagues, teachers, mentors, and acquaintances to that list. Some people come into our lives for short periods of time, others for longer, and several are with us for the long haul. We are made to relate to others — it's part of our genetic makeup and a necessary survival skill. So, here's the biggie; why do we have so many relationship problems?

That's a very good question, considering the difficulties we face in this area, and the answer may surprise you. You see, 'bad' or 'unhealthy' relationships have more to do with you than with the other person. That's not me pointing a finger at you; it's an insight that will empower you to establish healthier relationships once you have read through this chapter. But it is going to take some re-positioning of your attitude towards others and a rethink of how you contribute to your relationships.

Go online and you will find thousands and thousands of blogs, articles, research papers, and inspirational videos by experts from all fields talking about how to establish healthy relationships. I've got to say that most of them seem to focus on the typical love/romance types, which may be because so many people struggle in matters of the heart. We will get to that subject a bit later, but it's not the only kind of relationship that people have problems with. Many are estranged from their parents or children, experience high levels of conflict or toxicity in the workplace, and there are also a lot of us who can't seem to establish any kind of meaningful relationship with others whatsoever.

The Beatles once said that 'all you need is love', but that's not quite right. You need a whole skill set to establish strong, healthy relationships that are enriching and meaningful. There is so much literature about what makes a good or bad relationship and different theories on how to improve on them that I could fill another book on the subject. But for the purpose of this one, which focuses on self-love, we are going to take a closer look at setting boundaries and how to deal with toxic relationships. You may have experience of the latter and know just how destructive they can be, or you could find it hard to set healthy boundaries with family or friends and this can cause a great imbalance in your life.

What is a relationship? Quite simply, it's an association, connection, interaction, and bond between yourself and other people. Broadly speaking, there are four main types: family relationships, friendships, acquaintanceships, and romantic relationships. You could have good or bad experiences with one or more of these, which contributes to how you approach new relationships. How we relate to others becomes a pattern that is set very early on in life and although not permanent, it can be extremely difficult to establish new patterns later on. Perhaps it is one of the hardest things to do because it requires a high degree of emotional intelligence and a sincere willingness to change if you feel the need to. That's why you are here though, so I know you are ready to go for it.

Family ties

This isn't a psychology book aimed at solving all of your issues, but you will find some advice further on that applies to all relationships, and not only to family members.

Our family ties are complicated and come in many different shapes and forms. While the ideal is to feel love and closeness with our relatives, this isn't necessarily the case. We don't always get the guidance and support that we need and may grow up with an absence of boundaries or discipline. This can cause a lot of insecurities in later life that lead us to form relationships for all the wrong reasons. For women, a lack of a positive male or female role model while growing up can make it difficult to know how to be a mother, wife, friend, and partner.

In a stable home, conflict is usually short-lived and part of the daily dynamic, but if it is constantly present, it can create an unhealthy feeling of insecurity and low self-esteem. It can even be adopted as the blueprint for our own relationships in adulthood. For good or bad, family ties are lifelong, so it's beneficial to work on making those relationships as sound as possible to give you a continued source of support.

Unfortunately, for a myriad of reasons, this isn't always possible. The question is, how do we react to negative relationships with family members and overcome their impact on our well-being and bonding abilities with others?

Close friends

How many good friends do you have? Are you closer to some than others? Does that matter? Unlike our family, which we are born into, we can choose our friends and they are usually people who we trust, respect, care about and confide in. This kind of relationship needs to be built on reciprocal honesty, trust, and loyalty because if they don't exist, the friendship will end after a while. We tend to feel closer to older friends but there are no hard and fast rules to this. At the end of the day, it all depends on how much you deem someone to be a true friend or not and you can choose to continue the relationship or end it if you feel betrayed, let down, or hurt by them.

Casual acquaintances

How many people do you meet regularly who are not friends or relatives? You could have neighbors who you say hello to every morning and never take it further than that. Possibly, you work with people that you don't know well at all but you are probably polite and courteous in such cases and don't have any particular conflict with them or emotional engagement.

Romantic relationships

This kind of relationship is the one that concerns many of us because it is an extremely intimate, emotional, and physical bond. In such a relationship, whether that be short-term or long-term, it must be reciprocal and can even be life-changing. Mutual attraction, a feeling of being in love, and the sense of a strong connection usually lead to an exclusive relationship in which both partners desire to share their lives together. The secret to successful romantic relationships is said to be love, trust, respect, support, acceptance, and shared interests, which often leads to having children together and a lifelong commitment. Well, it doesn't always work that way, as you know, but that's the general idea.

Perhaps because romantic relationships occupy all of our thoughts, emotions, and even hopes and dreams, they are so important to us and usually, we will do whatever it takes to make them work.

And that's the first problem. If one side is not as invested, trustworthy, or capable of committing to making a go of it, the relationship can become a minefield. Conflicts can easily arise, emotional pain can deepen and all sorts of insecurities can rise to the surface. In many cases, the relationship is based on an imbalance right from the beginning or can become toxic as it develops. In this case, one or both partners can exhibit behavior that is detrimental to the other and there is the potential for the relationship to become extremely harmful. It requires a substantial amount of hard work to turn this kind of issue into something healthy and often, the best option is to walk away from it altogether.

Toxic time-bombs

You may have developed a toxic relationship with a partner, family member, or even with a friend. It doesn't only happen in romantic relationships, although this is what most people think of when the phrase comes to mind. No, your interaction with your parents, siblings, or best friends can be described as toxic if they manifest certain behaviors. What is important to remember is that two people make up a relationship, so you are just as responsible as the other person for continuing it. To put it another way, it takes two to tango, and any negative relationship that you maintain is made up of two parts — you and the other person. So, what are some of the traits of a toxic relationship? Let's have a look at the bullet points below, and see if you relate to any of them:

- A toxic relationship is characterized by behaviors on the part of one partner that are emotionally and often physically damaging to the other.
- A toxic relationship damages self-esteem and drains energy by excluding mutual care, respect, and compassion.
- A toxic relationship is not based on an interest in the other's welfare and growth or a shared desire for each other's happiness.
- A toxic relationship is not a safe place. It is a breeding ground for insecurity, self-centeredness, dominance, and control.
- A toxic relationship can end up being very dangerous to one's emotional and physical well-being.

A lot of what I describe above can be very subtle at first. You may not notice certain behaviors at first, or give the other person the benefit of the doubt when they belittle you or try to demean you. After a while, as the cracks become more obvious, you may fear for your sanity or even your life and could feel controlled, unable to break free. If you are experiencing any of these examples in a romantic relationship, here's my advice — get out NOW!

You aren't going to change the other person's behavior and the longer you stay, the more you feed their toxic ego. Make no mistake; such relationships don't end well and at best, you will be left feeling stripped of your self-worth and esteem. This kind of damaging scenario can also be experienced with controlling friends and even colleagues so you need to be aware of that and seek help if you feel unable to deal with it alone.

When it comes to experiencing toxicity from a parent who has spent years trying to undermine, dominate or control you, you will need to make some pretty tough decisions. As an adult, you have the maturity to decide which people are causing you damage and need to remove yourself from their influence. That doesn't mean that you stop loving your mother or father, but simply that you refuse to be a part of this toxic tango that has been going on for so long. You may feel pressured to give in to emotional blackmail but if you want to practice self-love, the first thing you need to do is protect yourself from those who don't care about your welfare and are only interested in satisfying their own needs. That has to stop!

Women tend to come off worse than men in toxic relationships (although men can also be victims) and are more susceptible to domestic violence. Recent studies reported in **woman's aid org UK** show that *"women experience higher rates of repeated victimisation and are much more likely to be seriously hurt or killed than male victims of domestic abuse."* In addition, *"women are more likely to experience higher levels of fear and are more likely to be subjected to coercive and controlling behaviours."* Needless to say, it is vital that you seek professional help and support if you are a victim of domestic abuse.

You may experience some of the following and need to recognize those feelings for what they are: bad for your well-being, self-esteem, and happiness.

- You feel bad all the time
- You feel empty and weak
- You're forced into conversations where whatever you say is used against you

- You avoid saying what is on your mind to dodge conflict
- You find yourself having to make compromises all of the time
- You are afraid to say no to anything
- You are always made to feel in the wrong
- You feel that you are fighting to save this relationship alone
- You are the victim of physical or verbal abuse, or both
- You are witness to too much passive-aggressive behavior
- You can never resolve any of the problems
- You are made to feel culpable and guilty
- You have no privacy
- You are subjected to lying
- You have no say in any decision-making

In terms of trying to deal with a toxic relationship, there are some things you can do which may salvage the situation and if they don't work, reach for the door. Some examples of useful strategies are as follows:

- Showing a willingness to invest in the relationship
- Encouraging self-awareness and self-responsibility
- Shifting from a blaming to an understanding perspective
- Suggesting outside help

Often, toxic relationships occur when long-standing issues in a relationship remain unaddressed, and there are some strategies to help turn that around:

- Don't focus too much on past events and resist the urge to throw mud

- Try to see any underlying reasons why your partner may be acting in this way You aren't making excuses for them, but it will give you an insight into their trigger points
- Be open to therapy, either alone, or as a couple
- Find support by talking to a close friend or join a support group
- Practice positive communication instead of negative accusations and criticisms
- Take responsibility for your own actions in prolonging this unhealthy situation
- Be prepared to part ways

Instead of being a victim, it is important that you move on in your life, which can be very hard to do if you have suffered from a damaging relationship. It will take time, but the benefits are definitely worthwhile. Once you begin to feel stronger, you will be less likely to put yourself in that situation again in the future.

Being part of a couple is not always easy and there are bound to be differences of opinion and arguments from time to time. In the best-case scenario, it is these small tensions that can lead to a stronger, closer bond with a mutual desire to improve the relationship. Your happiness doesn't depend on someone else but it can be greatly enhanced if you are in a warm, loving relationship.

Codependency challenges

Years ago, women were economically dependent on their husbands or partners, in the days when it wasn't acceptable or usual to seek employment outside of the home. Thankfully, that has all changed, although it is still very common for women to find themselves in codependent relationships, in which they feel that they cannot function as autonomous individuals. There are many reasons why this may be the case, most of which are probably related to their upbringing. Perhaps you recognize yourself as you read these words and if that is the case, hopefully, you can take something useful away from these pages.

You may not realize that this even describes you and your relationship because you have never thought about it before, and that's fine. If codependency does resonate with you, I am going to provide you with some strategies to overcome it. Often, it is a role that women slip into, partly because they are influenced by gender-related expectations of what a wife or partner should be like, and partly because they haven't worked on their inner insecurities and fears.

Codependency is actually emotionally and mentally debilitating because it assumes that you cannot function from your innate self, and your thoughts and behavior are organized around another person. You may be greatly affected by another's behavior or even obsessed with controlling it. You may be manipulative or aggressive with your partner or take the role of a victim or martyr and he/she may do the same.

Some other manifestations of codependent behavior include:

- Feeling that your partner is overly giving, fixing, caretaking, serving, and speaking on your behalf
- Constantly having decisions made for you
- Feeling that your personal growth is being limited or an inability to be involved in your own life
- Suffering from conditions such as anxiety and depression
- Avoiding emotional or physical intimacy

Do you feel that you are experiencing any of the above in your relationship? You are not alone if you do, and not to

89

blame for getting into this kind of behavior pattern. It takes a lot of soul-searching to find out why you are putting yourself through this and being aware of your inner feelings is crucial if you wish to redress the balance. That's why self-love is so important because when you have it as your mantra, it will always act as an anchor, guiding you back to what is best for you.

If you can work through why you feel the need to surrender your independence and autonomy in a relationship, it will help you to create a healthier stance towards both yourself and your partner. Think of it like being on a sailing yacht which can easily be blown off course if you aren't in control. You need to be able to drop anchor now and again to avoid being totally lost at sea.

My friends Todd and Miriam had been married for 15 years. They used to express openly how they did everything together and wouldn't dream of doing anything apart, such as going on holiday without each other. They are the kind of couple who finished off each other's sentences, ordered the same dishes at restaurants, and even seemed to color-coordinate what they wore, (although I'm sure that was just a coincidence.)

It came as a great surprise to me when I heard that they were going through a divorce because they had always seemed to be the 'perfect couple'. When I caught up with Miriam recently, she revealed how stifled she had felt in the relationship, and how she was desperate to find her independence. It's a funny old world, but I can perfectly understand why she felt that way. You see, there are three units to a relationship — you as an individual, your partner as an individual, and both of you as a couple. When the 'couple' element overwhelms the 'individual' element, then you lose the part of you that relates to your identity.

This is a very common pattern in relationships and one that is difficult to undo yourself from if it happens to you. But it can be done. It involves understanding any attachment issues that you may have and taking a step back every now and again for an ID check. We all want to be in loving, secure relationships, but that doesn't mean having to sacrifice your wants, desires, and independence to attain that.

In a balanced relationship, warmth, compassion, and understanding are abundant. There is room for personal growth and an acceptance of the other's shortcomings. As both partners have a healthy level of self-esteem, no manipulation or conflict arises from insecurities. Forgiveness and apologies are common and a genuine effort is made by both to improve and enrich the relationship. Most of all, there are clear distinctions between you, your partner, and the couple that you are together.

This can only happen if you nurture your self-esteem, deal with your insecurities and develop confidence in your abilities and qualities. As you can see, it all comes back to how you feel about yourself again. This is the one abiding truth that you need to embrace if you wish to have a fulfilled, content life. Luckily, there are strategies you can adopt to increase your levels of self-love, and ultimately be more prepared to enjoy a loving relationship with someone else.

- Be assertive when you want to express your emotional needs and state them clearly without being aggressive
- Don't take things too personally. An off-the-cuff remark or comment isn't always a personal attack on you
- Don't slip into the victim role because you are not. You are responsible for your actions

- Be prepared to trust in your instincts more, and allow yourself to trust others too
- Accept your flaws and recognize that no one is perfect
- Be mindful of your inner dialogue and reactions to that
- Stay true to your core values and don't let them be overshadowed by your partner's values
- Be open to change and to work on self-improvement. No need to try to change others — that's not your job
- Take time each day to reflect, which can be in the form of meditation, or just sitting quietly for a while and allowing your thoughts to pass by, like fluffy clouds

As I said at the beginning of this chapter, mastering relationships isn't so much about changing or controlling others. It is more about being aware of yourself, acknowledging your values and needs, and being prepared to develop greater self-love. Once you have done that, you will find it much easier to manage all of the relationships in your life and to build strong, healthy bonds with others. Remember, you are your anchor on the sea of life; a role too important to leave to anyone else.

We are going to continue the theme of romance in the next chapter by looking at how to write a love letter to yourself. It may just be the most empowering letter you have ever written, so get your pen and paper ready!

Affirmation:

Having healthy and loving relationships with others begins with loving myself.

﷼ 8 ﷼

A LOVE LETTER TO
YOURSELF

"All I ask is that you accept a letter from me."
— *Gabriel Garcia Márquez*

When was the last time you wrote a love letter in which you expressed your most intimate thoughts and feelings?

Not that long ago, before instant messaging, emails, and emojis, you had to literally put pen to paper and write down how you felt about the love of your life. You then needed to physically post the letter or find a way to have it delivered to the recipient. People have been doing exactly that for centuries and there is nothing more romantic than sending or receiving a love letter.

When Florentino meets Fermina in the brilliant novel, *Love In The Time Of Cholera* by Gabriel Garcia Márquez, it's love at first sight. Desperate to express his feelings for her, Florentino tries to find a way to give Fermina a love letter. He finally manages to do so, and once she accepts it, hundreds more are written to her over the next fifty years. Even though the woman of his dreams had married someone else,

Florentino never lost hope that one day he and Fermina would be together.

That's the power of love, or, should I say, the power of the written word to someone you love. Interestingly, both sender and recipient benefit from the whole process: the sender can freely express their deepest emotions and the receiver is enamored by such heartfelt outpourings. It is a truly romantic gesture that cannot be substituted by smiley faces and quick 'Luv U 2" texts. It may sound old-fashioned, but the act of expressing love through writing can be very liberating as you pour out your heart.

Despite the brilliant new ways of communicating that the digital world has brought us, using a real pen and paper still holds great value, even if you are only writing to yourself. You may think that sounds silly, but more and more studies have revealed how much good it can do you. Assuming that you don't spend much time reflecting on your value as a person, what better way to give yourself a boost than by writing a love letter to yourself? It's a way to celebrate the most important relationship you will ever have!

Just in the same way that bonds with other people are nurtured and enriched by endearing words and expressions of affection, writing to yourself can help you to develop more self-love and raise your esteem. The wellness culture that we live in today focuses a lot on feeling good, and not only physically. Apart from eating healthily and doing exercise, we now know that it's important to see to our emotional needs. We often neglect to pay attention to these as we are either too busy taking care of others or not in touch with our inner self.

When you are on that hamster wheel, it's difficult to get a good grasp of why you feel unhappy or to explore aspects of yourself that need attention. There are many ways to reconnect with your true self, some of which I've mentioned in this book. Mindfulness, meditation, and journaling are just a few of the things that can help you in this process and they are incredibly useful.

By writing an amorous letter to yourself, you are going one step further: you are affirming your self-worth, expressing an appreciation of who you are, and recognizing the good within you.

It doesn't have to be a soppy, Valentine's Day-style message full of clichés, which would seem a bit weird, but it can be loving and compassionate. Usually, we depend on others to sing our praises and tell us how much they care about us. But it's only when we really believe in ourselves that we can grow, develop and flourish into the women we wish to be.

That's where reflective writing comes in, which can offer you some great insights and help you to:

- put your thoughts and feeling in order
- express strong emotions
- offer a different perspective
- recognize and celebrate your achievements
- recall fond memories
- explore your strengths
- provide encouragement
- increase well-being

With journaling, you are noting specific things about your thoughts, feelings, and so on. It's a way to gain clarity and reconnect with yourself, but a love letter is slightly different. Firstly, it will make you feel wonderful, just as it would if it came from a lover, partner, or admirer. Secondly, you don't have to aspire to do anything, achieve any specific goal, or follow a restricting line of thought. It's just an opportunity for you to give yourself love, which we all need.

Words are powerful things and the way we practice self-talk becomes the template for how we see ourselves. If you write down positive words about yourself, the brain readjusts and takes them as truths, which ultimately raises your level of wellness. It sounds almost too good to be true, but there is plenty of very credible research to prove this. If you can write down some words of endearment, not only are you exercising your brain and flexing its memory muscle, but you are also aiding the process of emotional healing and stress relief. Studies show how it can help when dealing with drug dependency, depression, anxiety, and overcoming traumatic experiences. It's even been used in a clinical environment to help women dealing with breast cancer, asthma, irritable bowel syndrome, and a range of other medical conditions. So, yes, there is power in words and more than we thought.

The beauty of it all is that it's easy to write down how you feel and you can do it anytime, anywhere. You don't need any special equipment or have to be tech-savvy and, as it is for your eyes only, you are free to say whatever you like. When I say writing, it is better to use a pen on paper and not a keyboard if you can avoid it because it doesn't offer the same benefits.

But let me give you some prompts and examples to help you get off to a great start.

Letters of love

1. **Choose your approach**

Buy yourself a nice writing notebook or use any loose paper you already have. Invest in a good pen that flows easily. Writing by hand is the best way to create your love letter but if you find it too much of a hassle, you can use the notes app on your smartphone or type it as a document on your laptop/PC. Whichever format you choose, the act of laying out your thoughts and feelings should be a positive experience.

1. **Select your spot**

Set aside some time during your week to write the love letter. Make sure you won't be disturbed for however long it takes and choose a place where you feel comfy and relaxed. It could be at home, in your favorite coffee shop, or at the park — anywhere that allows you to compose your thoughts and put them down. Do it with intention and from the heart, rather than seeing it as a chore.

2. **Writing to yourself**

You are writing a love letter to yourself, so you should use 3rd person, which means beginning with something like:

Dear (your name),

You are so special to me because...

It may seem strange at first, but once you try it, you will soon see how it helps to reduce anxiety and enables you to deal with your emotions in a calming way. And, it gets you to address yourself with tenderness and empathy; two things that may have been missing from your life until now.

3. **Decide on the style**

There are different ways to approach the letter and it's up to you how you go about it. You may just want to pour out onto paper whatever is in your heart at this moment and let it flow naturally. There are no rules to freestyling, as long as you keep it positive, upbeat, and self-appreciative. If you find that a bit daunting, there are other ways of doing it that are more focused. One of them is to write to your younger, or future self. Let's say that you are writing to the younger version of yourself. What kind of things would you like to tell them and what advice would you give them? If you decide to write to your future self, what would you say to give them encouragement, hope, and love?

The whole point of the exercise is to talk about the physical attributes or characteristics that you love about yourself unconditionally. You can talk about your qualities and strong points or mention your achievements and accomplishments. The person who you are describing (i.e., you) deserves praise and acknowledgment, so don't hold back — go for it!

4. Make a list

You may want to spend some time beforehand making a list of ten things that you love about yourself, or more if you can. These will reflect all of your amazing qualities and your list could look something like this:

- I'm loyal
- I'm great at maths/cooking/swimming
- I'm honest
- I'm creative
- I'm generous
- I'm hard-working
- I'm always punctual
- I'm brave
- I'm trustworthy
- I'm very friendly

What you are doing here is focusing on your strengths and not your weaknesses. You may be used to dragging yourself down but now it's time to pull yourself up. Whatever you include in your list, don't undermine each quality or take them for granted. You are special and need to believe that. Also, by avoiding negative self-talk you are bolstering your overall feeling of being worthy, and this is an essential part of self-love. Just because you are tending to your own needs, it doesn't mean that you love others any less because your potential for love is infinite — you have more than enough for everyone, including yourself.

Once you have made your list. Take some time to consider how each quality has benefitted you in some way, no matter how small. If you think about it long enough, you will find examples of occasions when being creative, for instance, had a positive effect on your life because it may, for instance, have enabled you to create artworks that decorate your home. Make a note of your reflections in the following way:

- Being loyal has benefitted me because it has earned me the respect of my close friends.
- Being great at maths means that I can sort out my financial matters on my own.

You can continue with your own list and once you have done so, be sure to honor those qualities by finding ways that are personally meaningful to you. For example, by saying something like:

- I will continue to dedicate some time to my creative side because it makes me feel very fulfilled.
- I will remind myself that I am fortunate to be good at maths because not everyone has that skill.

Accepting the parts of you that you don't love is OK too because everyone has their pet peeves. I may not like the way I am impatient, for example. However, by recognizing that this is a part of who I am, I can work on improving that, which will definitely reduce my stress levels. There is no point in hating yourself for any of your shortcomings and using them against you. This isn't a court of law and you aren't on trial for anything so avoid being judgmental and critical. By simply accepting your weaker traits, you can let go of them and release yourself from the need to be perfect.

Examples

To give you a better idea of how to write your love letter, below you will find some examples of my own letters. Yours doesn't have to be exactly like any of these and, since you are unique, you can express yourself any way that you like. Just be true to yourself and remember what the intention is here: to nurture your inner self and develop a deeper sense of self-love.

Example 1

Dear Rebecca,

I remember how you had so many hopes and dreams when you were younger, and I know how hard you have worked to achieve some of them. You should be proud of yourself for everything that you have accomplished because it hasn't been easy. You truly are a courageous woman who is capable of so much and I am very proud to have been right next to you every step of your journey. We've gone through many tough times and shared more than a few tears together, but I know that you are deserving of all the happiness there is in the world.

I will always be here for you and hold you close to my heart.

Much love...

Example 2

My dear Rebecca,

I wanted to write to you to tell you how much I love you. I may not say those words often enough, and I am sorry for that. Sometimes it seems that I have taken you for granted and not fully appreciated the caring person that you are. You have always shown kindness to others and been considerate of their needs, often ignoring your own along the way. I remember when your sister was sick and you never left her side until she was well again. Your loyalty and dedication are amazing and I know that there have been many times when you have felt lonely and unloved yourself.

You bring so much joy to others with your kindness and deserve to be happy. Let me tell you that you are very special and I love you from the bottom of my heart.

All my love...

I think you get the idea. It can be as long or as short as you like, and you can focus on whatever feels right to you. Use phrases such as:

- Dear (name)...
- I wanted to express my feelings because...
- I love you because...
- You are so special to me because...
- I'm so proud of you because...
- What sets you apart from anyone else is...
- I'm grateful to you for...
- My wish to you is that...

Use words of tenderness and affection when writing this letter and afterward, you can read it out loud as many times as you want to. Once you are done writing it, you can put your love letter in an envelope if you like and address it to yourself. Place it somewhere safe or private and read it whenever you feel like it. Cherish it as you would if it was from a lover, and may it be the first of many that you will write to yourself. Alternatively, fold it up and place it under your pillow or lay it on your bedside table so you can read it before you go to sleep at night. Treasure it as the most important letter you have ever received, because it is!

The pleasure you will receive from reading your love letter can only be matched by the joy and positivity it will make you feel about yourself. You can be your own Florentino, declaring your love for the most special person in your life. Many heartfelt love letters have been written throughout history, but none are more beautiful than the one that helps you to love yourself so don't hold back — start writing today!

(As for Florentino and Fermina, you'll just have to read the book to find out if all of those passionate love letters spanning more than five decades ever help to bring the couple together in the end!)

If you like the idea of doing something a bit different, why not romance yourself with a love poem instead? Poetry is an exercise that really gets you to focus on the words you use and stretches your imagination. Because it has some basic rules, poetry can stop you from drifting off the subject, which may happen when writing a letter. It is the language of love and there is nothing as touching as a poignant outpouring of poetic expression. You can choose one of your qualities and focus on that, extolling its virtues as you would of a lover.

It doesn't have to be up there with Shakespeare or a literary masterpiece and you don't need to be a great writer to declare self-love in writing. Keep it as simple as you like but make it compassionate, tender, and accepting. The point is to honor who you are and fall in love with yourself. Learning to do so takes time but with a little help and patience, you will eventually be able to fully embrace yourself and all that you are.

Apart from working on your inner thoughts and feelings, there are many practical ways that you can introduce more self-love into your life, and we will be taking a look at those in the final chapter.

Being good to yourself should be part of your daily routine and it can become a newfound habit that makes you feel wonderful, so get ready to learn how to do just that. In the meantime, fall in love with yourself by reciting the below affirmation as often as you can and say it like you mean it, straight from the heart!

Affirmation:

I love and accept all of me and loving myself comes easily and naturally.

❧ 9 ❧

PRACTICING SELF-LOVE

"Eat like you love yourself. Move like you love yourself. Speak like you love yourself. Act like you love yourself. Love yourself."
— *Tara Stiles*

L ove. It is infinite, boundless, and an essential part of our human experience. So why do we find it so hard to love ourselves?

The funny thing about love is that we give it to others unconditionally, yet impose a whole list of conditions on ourselves.

We accept someone else's flaws, weaknesses, and imperfections because we love them, but cannot forgive our own.

We support our partners, children, family, and friends through bad times but beat ourselves up when we make a mistake or fail.

We can be the most caring, compassionate woman in the world but hate many aspects of ourselves.

It's a paradox that we seem to accept, without digging a bit deeper to see why we are such bad self-lovers.

I think, by now, you have realized that a lack of self-love is linked to several things such as low self-esteem, lack of self-worth, and negative patterns of behavior that we have simply gotten used to.

The truth is that it's not easy for us to love ourselves because we don't believe we deserve it.

You may even feel that the only way to experience self-love is when you are loved by someone else, and that's a slippery slope because what happens when that person withdraws their love? Relying on other people to regulate your emotional state is like walking on quicksand — you never know when you are going to sink. No doubt, if you have suffered from a romantic heartbreak or parental rejection, you will know what I am talking about. It hurts and makes you feel unloved and unlovable.

You can pour out as much love as you want to others, but when that glass is empty, how do you refill it?

The practice of self-love is the answer. When I say practice, I don't only mean treating yourself to a spa day or buying a new pair of shoes (all great ways to give yourself a quick fix). It has to be more than that and begins from deep within yourself, at the core of who you are. In this chapter, you will find some ideas on how to achieve that, as well as practical tips that will help you to form daily self-love habits.

As I mentioned early on in this book, self-love isn't about being selfish, egotistical, or self-centered. If you have any feelings of guilt when considering self-love, leave them here, because they will only sabotage the process. And if your negative inner voice is still trying to put you down, switch it off. Come with a real desire to embrace all that you are and don't forget self-compassion, which is an essential part of your emotional well-being.

Self-love is an appreciation for yourself that grows when you support your physical, psychological, and spiritual growth. It means having a high regard for your own well-being and happiness. It means taking care of your own needs and not sacrificing them to please others. It means believing that you deserve more. Whatever is important to you can be included in your self-love agenda. For example, you may feel the need to:

- Be true to yourself
- Prioritize yourself
- Stop self-judgment
- Trust yourself
- Be nice to yourself
- Set healthy boundaries
- Talk about yourself with love
- Forgive yourself more often

These are internal thought patterns that you need to work on if you want to reach a level of self-love that makes you feel more content, balanced, and fulfilled. No one else is capable of giving you this— not your partner, best friend, parent, or even your children. It's down to you to nurture those feelings of confidence, self-esteem, and self-worth because if you leave it to anyone else, it just isn't going to work.

Being praised by your boss for a job well done is great, but that has nothing to do with how you really feel about yourself. Being surrounded by people who love you is a blessing, but they can't make you love yourself. It's up to you.

My friend Debbie had a wonderful husband who loved her more than anything else in the world. He was supportive, caring, and affectionate, telling her how much he loved her every day. I thought she was so lucky because this man obviously idolized her. Unfortunately, Debbie had grown up in a very dysfunctional family and had never been able to overcome her feelings of insecurity and low self-esteem. No matter how much her husband loved her, she didn't feel that she deserved it. In reality, he loved her more than she loved herself. It wasn't until she started to work through her issues with a therapist that Debbie was able to start on a path of real self-love. It took her some time, but the process of self-reflection and facing her inner doubts slowly helped her to reclaim a happy, fulfilling life.

You may be just like Debbie or know someone who is suffering from the same problem. Although it is always advisable to seek professional help if your life is being seriously affected by negative feelings, there are some things that you can do now to help yourself. Here are a few basics for you to consider:

- **Practice mindfulness**. Tune in to how you feel at this present moment and reflect on the thoughts that come into your head. What are your needs and wants?
- **Stay focused**. Consider what behavior is a repetition of habits going back to your past. Do you need to continue to behave like this? What purpose does it serve?
- **Nourish yourself.** Daily exercise, eating nutritious food, and getting a good night's sleep are numero uno.
- **Be vulnerable**. Being open to intimacy and developing more social connections can bring you joy.
- **Do things with enthusiasm**. Responsibilities and obligations aren't always fun, but if you approach them with a positive mindset, they won't feel like an extra burden.

- **Say no more often**. Be selective about when you say yes to someone and make sure you are not compromising your own well-being to please others.
- **Practice self-care.** Listen to your body, look after your appearance, pursue your passions, and eat healthily.

Self-love is nurtured when you practice self-care, looking after yourself physically, emotionally, socially, and even spiritually. Going to the gym every day is admirable, but if you neglect the other aspects of yourself, you aren't going to feel that all-embracing self-love. Giving in to your friends' needs may make you popular, but that does nothing to raise your self-esteem. A combination of all these elements is needed if you want to develop a deeper sense of self-love and below you will find some useful points concerning each aspect of your needs. These are daily habits that you can begin to apply now. You may not be able to do all of them at once, but there are definitely quite a few that you can add to your daily routine relatively easily.

Emotional Self-Care

- Schedule some 'me' time into your daily routine
- Reward yourself when you complete small tasks
- Learn something new to upgrade your skills
- Develop a ritual of relaxation before you go to bed
- Allow yourself to express how you feel
- Use mindfulness exercises to bring you to the present moment
- Release stress or anxiety with jigsaws, crosswords, or adult coloring books
- Make a gratitude list of all the things you are thankful for

- Allow your feelings to be present without judging them
- Don't listen to the harsh inner critic inside your head
- Allow yourself to make mistakes

Physical Self-Care

- Do some stretching exercises when you wake up in the morning
- Go for a daily walk
- Drink more water
- Give yourself a good physical workout
- Go for a massage
- Spend 10 minutes under the sun if you can every day
- Spend some time in nature by hiking, walking, or cycling
- Get at least 7 hours of sleep each night
- Eat nutritious food and cook more often if you have time

Social Self-Care

- Avoid toxic people. This is a high priority!
- Ask for help. It's OK to admit that you aren't superwoman
- Talk to a friend or family member who you can trust
- Spend your time with people who are enthusiastic and positive
- Reconnect with an old friend and arrange to meet up
- Join a support group for people with whom you may share the same problems
- Schedule a regular night out with friends
- Invite siblings or other family members for dinner
- Have some fun

Spiritual Self-Care

- Put meditation on your daily schedule, even if it is just for 10 minutes at a time
- Do a 10-minute body scan to check in with each part of your body
- Do something nice for someone in secret
- Donate to your favorite charity
- Help someone in any way that you can
- Find a niche for your strengths or skills that benefits others

Once you realize that you are important, you will be more likely to adopt habits and behaviors that nurture your well-being and this, in turn, deepens your level of self-love. Be patient with yourself and accept your failings without feeling that you are worthless. Instead, shower yourself with understanding, compassion, and kindness, just as you would with anyone else you care about.

Self-love and bad behavior

We are all guilty of making one huge mistake: we judge ourselves based not on our inner being but on how we behave.

Instead of accepting ourselves, warts and all, we measure ourselves by what we did or didn't do. Full self-acceptance is unconditional: it means that we love ourselves regardless of how we behave, whether or not people approve of us or love us. We don't feel any less for our weaknesses and failures, nor do we feel better than others because of our successes. Self-acceptance is at the core of our relationship with ourselves and we should be more aware of that as we progress.

Evaluating our behavior is something quite different, but it seems that we pay far too much attention to it. We immediately believe we are a bad person if we don't help a friend or are too busy to visit a relative. It's not that we are masochistic (although sometimes you would believe so). We are simply too eager to berate ourselves when we make a mistake and take this far too personally.

Acting badly does NOT make you a bad person and condemning yourself to damnation is very self-destructive.

The other day, I accidentally scratched the fender of another parked car when leaving the office. Being in a hurry and with no owner in sight, I took a note of the registration number, intending to call later to exchange insurance details. Unfortunately, by the time I got home, I had lost the piece of paper and didn't know what to do. Apart from feeling frustrated, I also began to sense a feeling of complete disdain for my actions, telling myself that I was a terrible person. Yes, I converted my innocent accident into one of self-loathing in a split second, unaware that I was doing so until I stopped to think.

It's often a snowball effect, where one mistake can build up into a very damaging avalanche of self-hate. In reality, I know I am an honest and caring person, and I try to keep that at the forefront of my mind when self-doubt attempts to creep in. Regardless of any mistake or shortcomings, I aspire to self-love and tell myself every day that I am worthy. (Eventually, I did find the piece of paper in my bag and contacted the owner to settle the accident.)

So, how can you differentiate between rating the 'self' and rating your behavior concerning any past mistakes or regrettable actions?

1. Understand that you are not a bad person just because you act badly.

2. Identify your weaknesses without being defined by them.
3. Accept you have faults that you can work on correcting.
4. Don't attach blame or be over-critical of yourself when you make mistakes.
5. Know that you are 'enough' and worthy of love, despite any shortcomings.

We all make mistakes and are often far too hard on ourselves. Part of learning to love yourself is about letting go of those feelings of inadequacy, incompetency, or unworthiness because beating yourself up is actually bad for your mental and emotional health. Instead of feeling flawed in some way because you failed to do this or that, see it as an inevitable part of being human.

One way to get into this train of thought is to make a list of 5 things that you are not proud of from your past. It could be anything from forgetting your mother's birthday to snapping at another driver or being bad-tempered with a friend. When you have listed 5 past events, make an evaluation of yourself as a person based on each of the examples you have noted. Then, make a list that evaluates both you and the behavior. What personal characteristics would explain your behavior? Your list should look something like this:

Past mistake/event

Evaluation of self

Evaluation of behavior

Forgot mom's birthday

I'm a terrible daughter

That wasn't very thoughtful of me

Snapped at driver

I'm a nasty person

My reaction was over the top

Bad-tempered with friend

I'm a lousy friend

My behavior was uncalled for

Once you remove yourself from the equation and focus purely on your behavior, you can develop a much healthier perspective on things and not feel that you are a terrible person or a lousy friend. While you may strive to always behave the best you can, there will be times when you react badly and this is normal. It doesn't make you a lesser person, as long as you realize that your behavior was wrong and learn from your mistakes.

This is an important aspect of developing self-love: the ability to stay true to your inner core and not be pulled into negative self-talk just because you were out of line or behaved badly. And, you know something? Those people who were at the brunt of your bad behavior will probably forgive you very easily. You should do the same with yourself.

Being good to yourself

Being good to yourself should be on your daily list of things-to-do. It's not a luxury or a selfish act. It is an essential requirement if you want to lead a happy and fulfilling life. Below you will find **10 key habits** that will make you feel better about who you are and help you to love yourself unconditionally:

- **Be someone who loves**

Let yourself be open to loving others around you and loving doing specific things. Think about why you love being with certain people or why you love to walk in nature. Focus on what you appreciate about eating out, or going on vacation and let those positive emotions run through you. Feeling love is a truly empowering emotion.

- **Think about what it is to be loved**

Bring to mind a close friend or relative who loves you. If they were asked why, what would they say? Maybe they would mention your great sense of humor or your ability to show compassion. Whatever it is, hold on to that and enjoy being loved for all the reasons you can think of.

- **Stop comparing yourself to others**

Instead of magnifying your imperfections in comparison to someone else, accept that you are who you are and that's good enough for you. You may want to be 1,75 meters tall but you are only 1,65 and always will be. Comparing yourself to taller women is only going to make you feel miserable and I'm sure you don't want to feel like that. Instead, spend your time and energy nourishing your own sense of pride and worth.

- **Reset your emotional navigator**

The next time you feel bad about something, stop and ask yourself, "Why do I feel this way? What can I do to move forward?" Once you ask these questions, you may be surprised at the answers that come up. Our emotions can quite often be triggered by seemingly trivial events and are merely the outer layer of something much deeper. When you ask questions, you set off a process of investigation and very often discover that it's the underlying cause that you should be focusing on. By resetting your emotional navigator to what is really bothering you, you can learn to address the issue directly, instead of letting reactive emotions run away with you.

• Be with positive people

Spend time with those who you enjoy being with; those who make you feel good about yourself. Hang out with friends who are supportive and inspire you and if they don't, there's no need to devote all of your free time to them. It's better to surround yourself with positive acquaintances than friends who have nothing to offer you. Choose who you spend your free time with wisely and make sure it is because you want to be with them, and not just out of a sense of duty or obligation.

• Don't kick yourself when you are down

You wouldn't do it to someone else, so be kind to yourself when things aren't going your way. This is the time to be more loving and forgiving with yourself than ever and if you are feeling hurt, rejected, disappointed, lift yourself up instead of saying, "I told you so." Tend to your needs and be kind, just as you would with a stranger who needed your help.

• Develop healthy habits

This is a biggie and I don't need to explain to you the benefits of developing healthy habits for mind, body, and soul. Eat well, take daily exercise, and look after yourself. Although all three sound so easy to do, they are often the things that we neglect the most often. Eating well is a no-brainer and your body will thank you for it. Daily exercise may not sound very enticing, but even a walk around the block is better than nothing. Looking after yourself includes everything from personal hygiene to a top-to-toe beauty treatment and everything in between.

• Accept your imperfections

If you can love your imperfections, you are heading in the right direction. Dislike your lack of patience? Fair enough, but unless you can change that, it's not going to go away anytime soon. You may do well to remember that perfection lies in imperfection and that's what makes each one of us unique. Self-love isn't about having blind spots when it comes to your good and bad points. It's about accepting them and still being able to say, "I'm amazing."

• Let go of the past

You can't move on if you are dragging around a weight of emotional baggage from the past. As difficult as it may seem to let go, you must. Sometimes, past traumas are so deeply embedded within us that they feel like a part of who we are. They are not. They are dead weight dragging you down so the sooner you decide to let go of them, the better. You may need professional support or guidance to achieve this and it's perfectly OK to seek that out. You aren't a donkey and don't need to burden yourself anymore with events that happened long ago. You can be free.

• Be grateful every day

When you express gratitude for all of the good things in your life, you will feel happier. It's a well-known fact that people who focus on all the good things they have are more likely to be positive and optimistic, and exhibit a high level of well-being and self-esteem. Use gratitude as a daily tool if you are suffering from depression, a bad break-up, a career failure, or even in recovery from an illness or addiction and you will soon restore faith in yourself again.

Life is a rollercoaster ride of ups and downs and things never go in a straight line. One day we may be up in the clouds and the next, down in the dumps. Life just happens, from being healthy to falling ill, being head over heels in love to being broken-hearted. It's all part of the journey. But whatever happens, self-love is vital because when your foundations are rock solid, life is much less of a struggle.

You can be happy with what you have and loved for who you are. It's not something complicated but it does need practice. And, as you know, practice makes perfect. Spend more time on 'you', treat yourself to some tender love and care, and be compassionate when you fall short. Feel the love inside you and nurture it every day, letting it lead you to happiness and contentment.

Be the love of your life and live the life that you love. You have the power!

Affirmation:

The more I practice loving myself every day, the more love I receive in my life.

LOVE YOURSELF TRULY,
MADLY, DEEPLY

At the beginning of this book, you may have been unconvinced about the possibility of loving yourself. Maybe life has dealt you such a bad hand that it has left you feeling pessimistic about your future. Pain, trauma, and bad experiences could have completely exhausted your emotional reserves and it's possible you have been neglecting yourself for a long time while caring for others.

I hope that after reading each chapter, you discovered a woman who is worthy of love, respect, admiration, and compassion. I hope you discovered yourself.

We have looked at what it means to be a woman in today's world and the challenges that we face. Issues such as self-loathing in the face of external demands to be perfect are hard to overcome, but we looked at strategies to improve our sense of self-worth, putting our positive qualities first and foremost. You will recall that we found ways to deal with our negative inner critic and how to use positive self-talk to our advantage.

A lot of the themes running through the book have been related to raising our self-esteem and feelings of being worthy, something that I know many people struggle with. Most of our negative self-perspectives have to do with demoralizing self-judgment and we saw a variety of reasons why we need to let go and accept ourselves for who we are instead of indulging in self-criticism. We discussed why many women have adopted the bad habit of self-sabotage and learned a lot about the importance of changing our mindset.

Our body is beautiful, whatever shape or size, and we looked at how that fact can be reinforced, despite the enormous temptation to constantly compare ourselves to the unrealistic stereotypes in the world of social media. We looked at why it is essential to make ourselves a priority if we wish to find true inner balance, with many practical suggestions to achieve that.

We explored the different kinds of relationships and I have provided you with a range of strategies to help you form healthier, more meaningful ones that don't infringe on your sense of happiness. I have also given you lots of tips on how to manage toxic relationships that I hope you will implement immediately. We even delved into the language of love, where I explained how useful it can be to write love letters to yourself; a habit that is truly empowering.

Finally, we took an in-depth look at how essential self-love is to our wellbeing and the last chapter contains a wealth of advice on how to make self-love a habit, with lots of useful tips you can use every day.

You have been very brave as you read this book.

You have faced your fears, doubts, and insecurities.

You may have cried, laughed, or done both at the same time

You may have recalled events from your past that you had forgotten about.

You may have felt emotionally moved or challenged.

You may have recognized yourself in some of the examples.

You may have confronted issues that you had been pushing aside.

You may have found it stimulating, inspiring, and eye-opening.

My one wish is that you have found self-love!

Before you go, I want to leave you with the key essentials you need to enjoy a full and balanced life:

1. Stop comparing yourself to others

2. Stop worrying about other people's opinions

3. Allow yourself to make mistakes

4. Remember your value doesn't lie in your appearance

5. Walk away from toxic people and relationships

6. Face your fears

7. Stay true to your values

8. Practice self-care

9. Make yourself a priority

10. Be kind and compassionate to yourself

11. Stop judging yourself

12. Stop the self-sabotage

13. Set boundaries and say 'no' more often

14. Develop healthy habits

15. Practice gratitude on a daily basis

16. Bring mindfulness and meditation into your life

17. Spend more time with loved ones

18. Tune in to your emotions

19. Forgive your flaws

20. Enjoy life

Even if you don't manage to apply all of the above, think about all of the things you have overcome in your life. You are still here, full of a powerful feminine energy just waiting to be released. It takes time, so be patient with yourself and trust in the process. You are capable of achieving anything that you set your mind to so don't worry; you will get there eventually. You may struggle along the way, but one day you'll look back on these moments and feel a great sense of pride in what you have accomplished.

This is just the beginning of your journey and I hope you will use the strategies in this book to transform into the wonderful, strong, beautiful woman you really are inside. If, after reading each chapter, you have learned something about yourself, gained some small insight into how to increase your self-esteem and raise your confidence levels, then that's fantastic. You now have the tools to achieve the life that you have always dreamed of, on your terms.

I wanted to end with a brilliant and touching quote by Toni Morrison, the award-winning author. May you find something that resonates with you in her words:

"You think because he doesn't love you that you are worthless. You think that because he doesn't want you anymore that he is right — that his judgment and opinion of you are correct. If he throws you out, then you are garbage. You think he belongs to you because you want to belong to him. Don't. It's a bad word, 'belong.' Especially when you put it with somebody you love. Love shouldn't be like that. Did you ever see the way the clouds love a mountain?

They circle all around it; sometimes you can't even see the mountain for the clouds. But you know what? You go up top and what do you see? His head. The clouds never cover the head. His head pokes through because the clouds let him; they don't wrap him up. They let him keep his head up high, free, with nothing to hide him or bind him. You can't own a human being. You can't lose what you don't own. Suppose you did own him.

Could you really love somebody who was absolutely nobody without you? You really want somebody like that? Somebody who falls apart when you walk out the door? You don't, do you? And neither does he. You're turning over your whole life to him. Your whole life, girl. And if it means so little to you that you can just give it away, hand it to him, then why should it mean any more to him? He can't value you more than you value yourself."

By exploring the many ways that you can nurture self-love in your life, may this book be a stepping stone for you to find true happiness, starting today!

As you continue on the path to becoming the woman you were always meant to be, I will be with you each step of the way. Now that you have learned how to nurture self-love, explore more aspects of living a happy life by reading my next book.

Love Yourself Deeply is also available on Audible. Listen in the car, at home or even in the gym.

Free for you.

10 Weekly Issues of Rebecca's life-changing newsletter "Reclaim Your Power" Rebecca covers Self Love, Self Esteem, Making Friends, increasing your confidence and getting your life back, & Living a Life of Freedom.

https://rebecca.subscribemenow.com/

Other books by Rebecca Collins, on the next page.

How to Make Friends Easily

The Art Of Manifesting Money

Positive Life Skills For Teens

Make An Author Happy Today!

I hope you found this book helpful. If you did, I would be eternally grateful if you could spend a couple of minutes writing a review on Amazon.

When you post a review, it makes a huge difference in helping more readers find my book.

Your review would make my day

Thanking you in advance

Rebecca

SELF-LOVE JOURNAL

Keep a record of 3 acts of self-love every day for 7 days.

Before you go to sleep each night, think of 3 things you did today to nurture self-love. They can be anything from simple acts such as correcting your negative inner voice to saying 'no' instead of 'yes' when asked to do something you would rather not.

This journal-keeping will help you to acknowledge all of the positive steps you are taking towards true self-love and stop you from focusing on negative aspects of your life. After the first week, you can keep on writing in a notebook and make it a regular part of your daily ritual.

Day 1

1

2

3

Day 2

1

2

3

Day 3

1

2

3

Day 4

1

2

3

Day 5

1

2

3

Day 6

1

2

3

Day 7

1

2

3

SOURCES

https://www.nationalgeographic.com/science/article/
prehistoric-female-hunter-discovery-upends-gender-role-
assumptions

Prehistoric female hunter discovery upends gender role
assumptions, National Geographic, 2020

https://www.bbc.co.uk/programmes/articles/
1dRznJkKZ6DnGofXMD2hxNP/catalhoyuk-an-example-of-
true-gender-equality

The Ascent of Women, BBC Programmes/Articles

https://www.thebodyshop.com/en-us/about-us/activism/self-
love/self-love-index/a/a00043

Body Shop, The Self-Love Index Report, 2020

Brizendine, L., MD, The Female Brain, Harmony, 2007

http://amplifyyourvoice.org/u/marioapalmer/2013/05/21/byob-
be-your-own-beautiful.

5 Facts About Body Image, Palmer, M. Amplify, 2014

http://rebootedbody.com/038/

What Girls Are Taught About Health and Fitness (Round-table), Geary, K, The Rebooted Body, 2014

http://www.anad.org/get-information/about-eating-disorders/eating-disorders-statistics/

National Association of Anorexia Nervosa and Associated Disorders. 'Eating Disorders Statistics', ANAD, 2014

http://www.surgery.org/media/news-releases/survey-finds-that-women-are-more-likely-to-consider-plastic-surgery-than-they-were-ten-years-ago

ASAPS: The American Society for Aesthetic Plastic Surgery. 'Survey Finds That Women Are More Likely To Consider Plastic Surgery Than They Were Ten Years Ago, 2014

https://www.mentalhealth.org.uk/publications/body-image-report

Body Image: How we think and feel about our bodies, Mental Health Foundation, 2019

https://pubmed.ncbi.nlm.nih.gov/22229930/

A pilot study of expressive writing intervention among Chinese-speaking breast cancer survivors, Lu Q, Zheng D, Young L, Kagawa-Singer M, Loh A. Health Psychol, 2012

Made in United States
North Haven, CT
24 May 2022

19505985R00085